MORE HIDDEN TREASURES OF SANTA CRUZ COUNTY

Betty Barr

MORE HIDDEN TREASURES OF SANTA CRUZ COUNTY

Betty Barr

BrockingJ Books Sonoita, Arizona

To contact the author or order
additional copies of this book
write to us at:
P.O. Box 226
Sonoita, Arizona 85637
www.BrockingJbooks.com

This edition was prepared for printing by
Ghost River Images
5350 East Fourth Street
Tucson, Arizona 85711
ghostriverimages.com

On the cover: Shipping cattle from the Sonoita stockyards in the early 1950s. The photo was taken by Mary Boice of the Empire Ranch with one of the first Polaroid cameras.
Photo courtesy of Mary and Frank Boice family and the Empire Ranch Foundation

Back cover photo of the author by John Barr

ISBN: 978-0-9790261-3-3

Library of Congress Control Number: 2008909989

Printed in the United States of America

November, 2008

10 9 8 7 6 5 4 3 2 1

Contents

Dedicated to Patti Newmeyer Kelly

Editor, sister and best friend

Acknowledgments

Mere words are not adequate to express the extent of my appreciation to the many families who shared their memories and priceless photographs with me. Without their help, support and enthusiasm, this book would never have come into being.

A special thanks to those who may not have been relatives of the subjects of this book, but whose interest in the history of Santa Cruz County was invaluable to me. Kathy Mayo invited me to attend a reunion of the Little Outfit Ranch School and opened my eyes to a part of the west that is almost forgotten, Don Dean shared his extensive photo collection from the days when he was a student at the Little Outfit, Paige Gaylor sent me copies of old newspaper accounts that helped with the story on Fay Adams and Marka Collie Moss and Jane Collie Woods cheerfully answered my endless questions about anything and everything that happened in this county during the 1900s.

Laura López Murphy helped me with my sketchy Spanish and kept me grounded on Mexican history. Thanks also to Alison Bunting, Susan Hughes and the Empire Ranch Foundation for their generosity and willingness to share their notes and treasured photographs and to the Bowman Archives Center for the use of oral histories that made it possible to write about people who made an impact on the community.

Thanks to Dr. Paul Duffey, Kathy Nell Mayo and Steve Lindsey for allowing me to use their poetry. Their voices added a lyrical note to the stories about Blain Lewis, Slim Mayo and Lon Parker.

I was truly fortunate to have the assistance of two dedicated proofreaders and editors. Bob Bowman's knowledge of the people and the history of Santa Cruz County was invaluable in helping me keep things historically accurate and Patti Kelly's sharp eye and attention to detail prevented many of my mistakes from making it to print.

I would also like to thank Bob Kimball, former editor and publisher of the Nogales International/Bulletin, for his support of my work over the past ten years and for writing enthusiastic book reviews and arranging speaking engagements for me over the years.

Several of the stories on the following pages have appeared previously in the Nogales International/Bulletin newspapers, a division of Wick Communications Company. My heartfelt thanks to the company and to Manuel Coppola, editor and publisher, for their interest in publishing historical features in the local press.

Early settlers built this house into the side of a hill in the San Rafael Valley. The long-abandoned home is a testament to the hard work and perseverance of the pioneers who tamed the land and settled Santa Cruz County.
Betty Barr photo

Foreword

With the publication of Hidden Treasures of Santa Cruz County in the fall of 2006, it was soon obvious that I had barely scratched the surface in my attempt to capture the memories and histories of the early day settlers whose pioneer spirit forged the unique character of the county as we know it today. More Hidden Treasures attempts to pick up where the first book left off and include other pioneer families from Nogales to the west, the San Rafael Valley to the south and Patagonia, Elgin and Sonoita in the eastern section.

A few of the early residents settled just across the county line but, due to the remote locations, had greater ties not only in friendships and neighborliness, but also in commerce, with their nearest towns in Santa Cruz County. Their stories fit seamlessly into these accounts of early life in this area. A few examples are the Thurber Ranch, Greaterville and the Empire Ranch north of Sonoita and the Caviglia family, who homesteaded in Arivaca, south and west of Amado, all located in Pima County, and parts of the story about Slim Mayo that were set in Cochise County.

The earliest inhabitants were a diverse group. Indian tribes, Spanish explorers and missionaries, gold-crazed miners, adventurous military men, Mexican and Chinese laborers and finally, the westward-moving pioneers and homesteaders all contributed, in his own unique way, to the formation of the county.

Spanish explorer, Fray Marcos de Niza came north from Mexico through the San Rafael Valley near Lochiel in 1539 and was purportedly the first European to enter Arizona. Francisco Vasquez Coronado arrived the following year. His adherence to the Spanish policy of Indian murder and enslavement is generally credited with sowing the original seeds of hatred for the European in the southwestern Indian tribes.

In 1691, Father Eusebio Francisco Kino, a Jesuit missionary and explorer, entered into Arizona through the San Rafael Valley, continued over the Canelo Pass to the Babacomari River and first saw the peaceful Pima Indian farming tribe known as the Huachucas near present day Elgin. Father Kino introduced cattle into the Santa Cruz Valley and established several ranches.

Warring Apaches drove many early settlers away, but when Mexico gained independence from Spain in 1821, new land grants were created to encourage settlement in the area. The Baca Float combined the old Tumacacori, Calabasas and Guevavi grants into a ranch of 100,000 acres. Other early land grants included the San Rafael de la Zanja, San Jose de Sonoita, Babacomari and Canoa. Many of the grants remained abandoned after the Civil War and squatters moved in, built houses and operated cattle ranches, although they did not hold official title to the land. Eventually, the Mexican grants were sold to Americans and the squatters were forced to move.

Ft. Buchanan was abandoned during the Civil War and the Apaches, no longer fearing punishment, raided at will for the next 30 years, driving many miners, ranchers and farmers from the area. The Apache wars finally ended with the capture of Geronimo in 1886.

The "Y in the Road" was a meeting place for ranch families in the 1940s. It was located near Mustang Corners, at the present day intersection of Highway 92 and Highway 82.
Photo courtesy of Kathy Nell Mayo

The Homestead Act of 1862 encouraged westward migration. For a $10 filing fee, any citizen, man, woman, slave or freeman, could claim 160 acres. To "prove up" on the claim, the applicant had to be 21 years of age and was granted five years to live, build a dwelling on the land, make improvements and plant at least 40 acres with some kind of crop. By 1881 the Santa Fe Railroad extended their tracks 88 miles to meet up with the Mexican train coming from Sonora to Nogales. The railroad was a boon to the farming, mining and ranching communities and also boasted passenger service. There were two trains a day, one for freight and one for passengers.

By the early 1900s, the county was dotted with one-room schools, mining and ranching enterprises were flourishing and families rode miles over rough terrain on horseback, buggies or wagons to meet up with their far-flung neighbors for picnics, dances and church services.

This sequel attempts to relate the memories of days gone by while they are still fresh in the minds and hearts of those whose ancestors settled in the area during the past hundred years and more. Even so, there are countless other stories hidden in the hills and valleys of this vast and beautiful land, waiting to be told another day.

Walter L. Vail, owner of the Empire Ranch, at age 30. Ca. 1881.
Photo courtesy of Laura V. Ingram and the Empire Ranch Foundation.

Walter Vail

"There's a big ledge, and the whole dammed hill is a total wreck with quartz boulders of ore," Jerry Dillon told his employer Walter Vail as the two were riding the range on the Empire Ranch in 1879. Vail and his brother Ned along with Dillon immediately staked out a mine. Vail called it the Total Wreck, filed a claim and set up a stamp mill to extract the silver at the mine, located in the Empire Mountains about eight miles north of the ranch headquarters.

Ned's hobby before he came west to join his brother Walter, was assaying. He was fascinated by the process to determine the value of precious metals and frequently visited an assay office in New York and assisted with calculations. He became the assayer for the Total Wreck. They built a house nearby for the mill man and Ned wrote, "He said he slept fine as long as the mill was running, but if for any reason it stopped, he was up there in a minute – anyone who has ever heard a quartz mill running would not consider it a lullaby to induce sleep."

The Vails laid out a townsite near the Total Wreck and sold lots. During its heyday there were about 50 houses and 300 residents, three stores, three hotels, four saloons, a brewery, butcher shop, bank and a lumberyard. The Vail Post Office was established there in 1881.

By 1883 the mine was at peak production, with Nathan Vail acting as general manager. Southern Pacific put rails to the new town to bring in supplies and carry out the ore. Nathan eventually set up a profitable toll road through the area that controlled the cattle trail to the Southern Pacific loading chutes at Pantano.

They extracted $2,000 worth of silver a day and had brought in $500,000 in total revenues by the time the mine closed in 1887.

Miners on scaffolding loading an ore car for transport at the Total Wreck Mine. 1887.
Photo courtesy Julia Scribner Ruch, Laura V. Ingram and the Empire Ranch Foundation

Walter Vail and his partner Herbert Hislop had purchased the first 160 acres of what was to become the Empire Ranch in 1876 from E. N. Fish and Simon Silverberg for $2,000. Hislop was a native of England and when John Harvey, another Englishman, joined the venture a few months later, locals dubbed the enterprise "The English Boys Outfit," despite the fact that Vail was an American.

After a few short years of ranching, both Englishmen sold out to Walter Vail; Hislip in 1878 and Harvey in 1881. Business had already started to boom when Ned Vail came west to join Walter in 1879. Proceeds from the Total Wreck added significantly to the ability of the Vails to keep the cattle ranch profitable during periods of drought and slumping cattle prices.

John Harvey, one of the "English Boys," with his horse, Billy, in the corral. Harvey, Herbert Hislop and Walter Vail were the original partners in the Empire Ranch operation. Ca. 1880.
Photo courtesy of Julia Scribner Ruch, Laura V. Ingram and the Empire Ranch Foundation.

The brothers had a vision and adhered closely to their plan to buy all the available acreage in the area, especially property that gave them control of the water rights. By 1881 the ranch was truly on its way to becoming an Empire, boasting more than 5,000 head of cattle.

Edward "Ned" Vail was the assayer at the Total Wreck Mine. Known as "Tio Ned" to his family, he died a bachelor in 1936 at age 87, after serving several years as President of the Arizona Historical Society. Ca. 1900.
Photo courtesy of Laura V. Ingram and the Empire Ranch Foundation.

Vail was now a prosperous rancher and was in a position to make the trip to his home back east to claim his future bride. He had improved the house from a bare adobe building with a dirt floor and no windows or doors, to one habitable by a civilized lady. He also added a huge Victorian bay window that he hoped would convince his fiancée's socially prominent family that he would not be bringing their daughter to a savage and uncivilized outpost. Walter Vail and Margaret Russell Newhall were married in Plainfield, NJ, and returned to the Empire where they lived until 1896 when they moved the headquarters to Los Angeles.

Margaret Vail, holding her two-year-old baby Margaret, in the doorway of Leon Conyers' Mescal Spring Ranch in the Whetstone Gap, just purchased by Walter Vail to control range operations in that area. Other children, from left: Walter Vail, Jr. (or possibly Russ Vail), Amy Schoefield, and Mahlon Vail. 1898.
Photo originally provided to Mary Vail by Harry Heffner, early ranch foreman. Photo courtesy of Christine V. Shirley, Laura V. Ingram and the Empire Ranch Foundation.

Walter often told the story of how he almost lost his life trying to defend a yellow dog named Billy, who had been included, along with the cattle, in the purchase price of the ranch. Billy liked to run under the tongue of Walter's butcher wagon, between the mules. One day, according to Walter, "a big dog jumped on Billy and was chewing him up. I picked up a stick and was beating the big dog off ...when the owner...came up and pulled out a gun. In a minute several men with six shooters drawn were facing each other and I was in the middle....Although I was scared, I felt most anxious to prevent a fight. I think I said, 'You men are all friends of mine, don't kill each other over a yellow dog.' One of them laughed and I said, "Come with me," and we all went into George's saloon and I paid for the drinks and that ended the trouble."

During a roundup on May 10, 1890 Walter spotted a beautifully marked Gila monster. He shot it and tied it on the saddlebag behind him. After riding a distance, he reached back to make sure it was still secure. His fingers went in the animal's mouth and the reptile that he thought was dead snapped its jaws shut

The Empire Ranch cook shows off the zaguan, or breezeway area, to a group of ladies visiting the Empire Ranch in the mid-1880s.
Photo courtesy Laura V. Ingram and the Empire Ranch Foundation.

Vaqueros on horseback lined up in the corral at the Empire Ranch headquarters while women and children look on in the background. Ca. 1890.
Photo courtesy Laura V. Ingram and the Empire Ranch Foundation.

like a vise. He rode several miles back to camp where ranch hands had to dissect the animal to free his hand. Someone sent a message for Southern Pacific to rush an engine to the mine to take him to Tucson, where he finally recovered after several weeks of treatment.

The arrival of Southern Pacific Railroad had opened up cattle markets outside the Territory and the Vails routinely shipped to Los Angeles and Kansas. When SP increased their rates in 1889, the Vails led a protest against the same rail line that had saved Walter's life during the Gila monster incident. The Vails decided to boycott the railroad and drive their cattle overland.

Ned, along with their foreman Tom Turner and eight Mexican ranch hands, drove 917 steers from the Empire to the Warner Ranch pastures in California in 71 days. They survived a stampede and a perilous crossing of the Colorado. They recaptured 110 runaway steers and encountered a challenge by Indians, who they appeased with sugar and coffee beans. They traveled the desert at night and hung a lantern on the tailboard of a wagon to guide the steers. They stumbled on cattle bones, rattlesnakes, a broken-down wagon and a human skull. In Yuma, the sheriff tried to arrest two outlaws who had joined the cattle drive and ended up killing one and taking the other to jail.

In spite of all these adventures, they had lost only two head of cattle while crossing the Colorado and made $4 more per head over the cost of shipping by rail. When the cowboys returned to Arizona, they met with other ranchers who wanted to identify a safe overland route so they could also ship by land. The route was never established because an SP representative attended the meeting and reduced the shipping fees to the previous rates.

Walter Vail served in the Arizona Territorial Legislature and was a Pima County Supervisor. He and his brother Ned were charter members of the Arizona Cattle Growers'Association in 1904 and were influential in establishing fencing regulations to help control cattle rustling.

Walter had acquired several ranches in California including Santa Rosa Island, now part of the National Park Service, and the family moved their headquarters to Los Angeles in 1896. However, he continued to travel back and forth to oversee the operations at the Empire. He was killed in a tragic accident in 1906 as he was getting off a streetcar. He turned to help his wife disembark when another streetcar came along in the opposite direction and he was crushed between the two. At this time his son, Banning Vail, 17 years old, was sent to Arizona to train at the Empire Ranch and in 1913 he became the manager.

The ranch is now owned by the Bureau of Land Management, which oversees the range as part of the Las Cienega National Conservation Area. The Empire Ranch Foundation, a non-profit group, provides educational programs and spearheads historic preservation at the headquarters. John and Mac Donaldson run cattle on the property through a lease arrangement. Nothing much remains of the Total Wreck Mine but a few crumbling walls and several mineshafts.

Harry Heffner, manager of the Empire Ranch, on horseback in the corral. The carpenter shop and bunkhouse can be seen in the background. 1896.
Photo courtesy Christine V. Shirley, Laura V. Ingram and the Empire Ranch Foundation.

Jim Kane was the 1928 Tucson Rodeo All Around Cowboy and won a $200 saddle.
His 6-year-old son, Grover, won best-dressed cowboy at the Parade.
Photo courtesy Ross Kane

James “Jimmy” Kane

Jimmy Kane could ride the meanest bronc to a standstill. He was so good, in fact, that at the weekly events at Kinsley’s Cow Palace in Amado in the early 1920s, he was known for breaking horses that no one else could ride. There was no permanent arena at Kinsley’s in those days, so everyone pulled their cars into a circle to make an area for the competition.

When Kane drew a particularly nasty bronc one day, the cowboys put silver dollars on the stirrups under his boots. Wealthy ranchers placed $100 side bets that the coins wouldn’t be there when Jimmy hopped off. When Kane successfully “rode him down” all the spectators honked their car horns in celebration.

Although he never competed outside of his home state, Jimmy Kane was named the All Around Cowboy at the 1928 Tucson Rodeo and won a $200 saddle. That same year, his six-year-old son, Grover, won an award for Best Dressed Cowboy. A plaque listing Kane as an inductee in the Santa Cruz Cowboy Hall of Fame hangs in the Cowbelles Ranchers’ Heritage Center in the Old Nogales Courthouse.

Jimmy was born in Pantano and spent his entire life in southeastern Arizona. He married Rose Farley when she was only 15 and he was 26. The Farley family came to Patagonia from Chicago by train in 1919. Rose’s father, John Farley, was a miner whose friend, Dan Dawson, had located in Patagonia and told him of the mining opportunities in the area. The family discovered later that Jimmy Kane was on the same train, returning from service in WWI, but Kane and the Farleys did not cross paths at that time.

Jimmy Kane in Patagonia 1928.
Photo courtesy Tom and Joan Kane Wood

Rose was a tiny girl, 4'10," and walked with a limp from an early battle with polio. Her father threatened to have Jimmy arrested because of her age, but the couple ran off to Nogales, told the clerk she was 18 and were able to obtain a marriage license. On their wedding night their friends held a shivaree and made Jimmy push Rose, dressed in her nightgown, down the main street of Patagonia in a wheelbarrow.

Catherine and John Farley with their children Francis, Mae and Rose in Butte, Montana in 1906. Rose Farley later married Jimmy Kane. Photo courtesy Tom and Joan Kane Wood

Jimmy was a Patagonia Deputy Sheriff and he and Rose ran the Santa Cruz Hotel. They had three children, Grover, Frances and Joan. Both Jimmy and Rose could trace their family roots back to pioneer days in the Sonoita/Patagonia area.

Business card: James G. Kane, Candidate for Re-election for office of Constable. Subject to Democratic primary election. Sept. 9, 1930.
Courtesy Tom and Joan Kane Wood

Jimmy's father, James Kane, came to Sonoita in 1883 on a cattle drive and went to work for the Empire Ranch. He was the foreman of that portion of the Empire near the Total Wreck Mine. He had served in the Confederate Army and when his first wife passed away after the war, Kane left his two children in the care of their grandparents and came west. The following year he met and married Mary Gardner, whose father, Tom Gardner, was also a pioneer and is considered to be one of the first white settlers in the area.

Tom Gardner farmed in Patagonia in 1857, at the same spot where the Patagonia Depot is now located. In 1860 Gardner married Gertrude "Tula" Apodaca in Santa Cruz, Sonora. Several years later, he started a farm on Sonoita Creek. The troops at Ft. Crittendon were charged with protecting the settlers from the

Brothers Jimmy, Joe and Henry Kane in front of the Fresno Saloon in Patagonia. The youngest brother, Bob, had not been born when the picture was taken. Later he got dressed up, although the other boys were in casual clothes, and they pasted his picture into the photo. Ca. 1915.
Photo courtesy Robin Kane Gierhart.

Apaches. When the creek ran dry in 1870 he bought place a few miles farther downstream and later homesteaded at Apache Springs and owned a sawmill in nearby Sawmill Canyon.

In the 1850s, Gardner was shot and wounded by Cochise and his band of Indians in Sonora, Mexico. He crawled into the thick mesquite and to keep from bleeding to death he stuffed his handkerchief and glove into his wound. His wife rode 30 miles on horseback to find him and nurse him back to health. Years later on a visit to Ft. Grant, Cochise came up to him and said, "Hello old fellow, I have been trying to catch you," and started to shake hands. Gardner answered, "I'll never shake hands with you, you old devil." This story has become a legend in the Gardner and Kane families.

Tomasa Gardner (right) as a young girl with her 13-year-old sister, Elizabeth. Tomasa later married William Dumont, superintendent at Salero Mine. Ca 1890.
Photo courtesy Tom and Joan Kane Wood

James and Mary Kane, Jimmy's parents, homesteaded at the mouth of Gardner Canyon, but sold out during the Depression, moved to Crittendon in 1898 and in 1900 to the newly founded town of Patagonia. Tom Gardner sold to the Vails in 1895 and joined his daughter and son-in-law in 1898 at the Crittendon townsite at Casa Blanca Canyon.

Jim Kane at Will Hathaway's Ranch on Duquesne Road near Nogales. Jim won the All Around Best Cowboy at the 1928 Tucson Rodeo, winning the third trophy saddle ever made by Porter's Western Wear for the rodeo. It was stolen from a warehouse in Tucson in the mid-1960s. Ca 1920s.
Photo courtesy Marguerite Lackey

Jimmy's parents ran a boarding house and restaurant in Patagonia. They had a Chinese cook named Frank, and a maid who helped them with the cooking. Although Mary went blind in 1907, she still took care of everything and ran the restaurant, even baking all the bread served. "Miners came off the train looking for work. There was only one other place around where people could get rooms and we were always busy. My father also ran a livery stable for people needing horses or rigs for getting up the canyon to the mines," Jimmy's sister, Grace Kane Chapman, said in an article in "Arizona National Pioneer Ranch Histories."

When Jimmy's mother was visiting at his home, he would string a clothesline from the back door to the outhouse so she could feel her way across the yard. The yard was filled with cows and chickens but somehow, even though she could not see, she managed find her way. Joan Kane remembers, "Grandma would touch our faces with her hand to see if we had washed. If she felt anything she would send us back for another scrubbing."

Jimmy Kane developed pneumonia and passed away at the Veteran's Hospital in Prescott in 1931 at the age of 38. He was buried in the Patagonia Cemetery. His widow, Rose, later married Dawson Scoggins who owned the Big Steer Saloon in Patagonia.

Grover Kane at the PO Ranch headquarters in Parker Canyon where he was the ranch manager for many years. Ca 1974.
Photo courtesy Marguerite Kane Lackey

Grover Kane

Grover Kane never went to high school, according to his sister, Joan Kane Wood. He told his parents that school gave him a headache and made him sick. They agreed to let him to drop out after 8th grade, and he immediately started his cowboy life. The lack of a formal education didn't seem to have an adverse effect on his future success, but he did miss out on lots of country fun Joan said.

On Saturday nights they had dances at the Patagonia Opera House with Alvessa Hummel and her band, including Jack Turner and Ed LeGendre, providing the music. The whole family, young and old would attend. Parents wouldn't allow the young people to go across the border to the dances in Nogales, Sonora but sometimes they would say they were going to the movies and sneak across the line instead. The Opera House, which Tom Gardner, Jr. built for Rollin Richardson, was also a great spot for roller-skating. A Chinese man from Nogales brought the skates, and the children who couldn't afford the admission brought gunnysacks full of firewood for the stove to gain entrance.

Grover ran away from home after his father, Jimmy Kane, died and his mother, Rose, married Dawson Scoggins, owner of the Big Steer Bar and Grill. Scoggins had previously owned the confectionary where the Wagon Wheel Saloon used to be located. The ice cream for his soda fountain came from Nogales. Howard Easley, a handsome young man, worked there. Some of the married ladies from Sonoita had a crush on Howard and would make the 24-mile round trip to Patagonia to buy ice cream, just for an excuse to talk to him. Years later, Grover opened his own bar, Kane's Cocktail Lounge, on Grand Avenue in Nogales, close to the international border.

Grover went to live with his uncle Joe for a time. Joe managed the T-4 Ranch, near Nogales. Shortly afterward, Grover hopped a freight train leaving Patagonia with a load of cattle, and at the age of 15 ended up in Sheridan, WY where he worked on a ranch and lived in a cow camp.

Grover Kane, age 6, won Best Dressed Cowboy, Tucson Rodeo Parade in 1928.
Photo courtesy Tom and Joan Kane Wood

Grover Kane with Nugget, by El Rey, by Man O' War at the Circle Z Ranch. At 6'2", Grover is dwarfed by the huge horse who measured at least 17 hands. Ca 1940s.
Photo courtesy Ross Kane

By the time he was 19, Grover was back in Arizona and working at the A-7 Ranch on the San Pedro River near Vail. He joined the Marines in WWII and left his cattle with Bob Bergier. When he returned, they had bred and he now had his own herd, which he immediately sold for cash. Soon afterwards he married his sweetheart, Marguerite "Tommye" Middleton of Rain Valley. She was the daughter of Ross Middleton, longtime manager of the Lone Mountain Ranch.

Grover spoke fluent Spanish and qualified for a job with the government to go to Mexico to help eradicate hoof and mouth disease in cattle. He and Tommye traveled to Mexico City along with Paul, his cousin, and Monte Jo Kane and

Austin and Marka Moss. They were there for three years.

From Mexico City, the men traveled to the wild state of Guerrero to test livestock for the disease. It was very backward and the only thing of value the people had was a few cows and a goat. The Indians treated their animals like members of the family, even bringing them inside the house to pen them up. To eradicate the disease, all the animals for miles in every direction had to be killed. "Their job was to go to remote places up in the Sierra Madres and basically tell people, 'We are going to ruin your life,'" according to Grover's son, Ross. For their protection, they were accompanied by armed guards, sometimes as many as 15 men, according to Austin Moss, furnished by the Mexican government.

Moss remembered one incident where a Mexican Indian had raised two oxen from babies. He taught them to kneel so he could wind a rope in a figure eight around their horns. He attached the rope to a bar and it served as a yoke to pull his plow. Before they had vaccines, all the animals on the premises, not just the infected cattle, had to be killed. It was not a happy or safe task to tell this man that his oxen would have to be sacrificed.

Paul Kane, Grover's cousin, later operated the Buffalo Corrals at Ft. Huachuca where he rented and boarded horses. He put on trail rides, cookouts, rodeos and gymkhanas. In the early 1980s, he returned to Mexico for the screwworm eradication program. Agents would fly over pasture areas that had infected cattle and drop out boxes full of sterile flies. The boxes had holes in them allowing the flies to get out and breed with the infected flies, eventually eradicating them. Paul was flying over the Sierra Madres on one of these missions when the plane hit a mountaintop, killing all on board.

When Patagonia incorporated in 1948, Grover was appointed the first official Town Marshal. He only stayed in the position for a few months because the town council decided they wanted to have their own fulltime lawman. Since Grover was already working as a Deputy Sheriff of Santa Cruz County, he turned the marshal position over to H.S. Reed.

Most of Grover's duties as Deputy Sheriff centered on controlling drunken brawls in the mining camps in the San Rafael Valley. He would load the drunks in the rear seat and take them to jail in Patagonia. There was no divider between the front and back seat. One night after a major brawl one of the miners was knocked out, either by Grover or the man he had been fighting with. The drunk came to on the way to Patagonia and as they drove by Harshaw, he leaned over the seat and started attacking Grover. "Dad told me that he was jerking the wheel

Paul Kane was killed in a plane crash when he was working to combat screwworm in Mexico in 1983 or '84. His plane hit the top of the Sierra Madres and all on board were killed.
Photo courtesy Ross Kane

this way and that, trying to stay on the road and keep from getting socked," Ross Kane said.

One of Grover's uncles was Vincent "Vin" Farley, a little Irishman who was a Justice of the Peace in Patagonia in the 1930s. According to Grover's daughter, Marguerite Kane Lackey, "He was too young to sign legal papers such as marriage licenses and death certificates. All he could do was arrest people and keep order." On the Fourth of July, Vin would go on a binge, along with a lot of other locals. He would fill the two rooms of the jail with drunks, then start handcuffing the others to posts and telephone poles. "The last one he would cuff would be himself," Ross Kane said. Vin's brother, Gordon Farley, was the longest standing Superior Court Judge in the United States when he retired after 38 years of service.

Grover Kane was a cowboy his entire life, with only a brief timeout working for his brother-in-law Tom Wood at Wood Bros. Lumber in Tucson. His wife Tommye worked in the Post Office at Ed LeGendre's store in the 1940s and Grover cowboyed on many ranches in the area, including the A-7 and the T-4. He was part owner and manager of the U/V north of Mayer in the 1960s. He was foreman of several ranches, including the Circle Z and a 13-year stint at the PO Ranch. "He spent his life doing what he loved best," his son Ross said. Grover passed away in 1996 at the age of 74.

Grover Kane, Dick Barkley and Bobo Chapman at the Circle Z Ranch where Grover was the manager. His son Ross worked there as a wrangler and later as manager for several years. Circa late 1940s.
Photo courtesy Ross Kane

Austin Moss on Keno at the Gill's Buenos Aires Ranch in Sasabe, Arizona. 1948.
Photo courtesy Austin Moss

Austin Moss

The year was 1933, the destination a remote mining community in Arizona known as Mammoth. Twelve-year-old Austin Moss, accompanied by his younger brother John and a friend he remembers only as "the Martinez kid," decided to run away from home and return to his father's old homestead in Ray on the banks of the San Pedro.

The three youngsters took off from the far north side of Tucson, near Pastime Park, and hoofed it 40 miles to Mammoth. John got discouraged during the long trek and turned back, but the two older boys got bread and sardines at the store, made sandwiches and fell asleep under a tree. They awoke to the sight of the county sheriff standing over them. Sheriff White delivered an ultimatum. The boys could either return home or go to jail. They headed for home.

Home for Austin was his grandmother's place, where a strap cut from his father's saddle hung on a peg by the door, handy when discipline was called for. His mother, Annie Daily Moss had died of peritonitis when Austin was about two, leaving 7 motherless children, including Austin and a new baby, John. A few years later his father, Charlie, a moonshiner, was killed when his truck, with a keg of homemade whiskey in the bed, ran off the road near Oracle.

After Charlie's death, the children were shuttled from one relative to another. By the time Austin was in fifth grade, he was living with an uncle in New Mexico. When the uncle came on hard times, Austin was returned to his grandmother where his aunt Mildred and her most recent husband were already living.

Austin didn't get along with Aunt Millie's husband and when he turned 15, he ran away for the second time, telling his grandmother, "I'm going to Amado and work for Byrd Yoas." His grandmother agreed not to send the cops after him and gave the teenager his inheritance – his father's split cowhide jacket, vest and bedroll.

Byrd Yoas at the soda fountain at the Owl Drug in Tucson where he often went to hire day workers for his Agua Caliente Ranch in Amado. Ca. late 1930s.
Photo courtesy Austin and Marka Moss

Toting these meager possessions, Austin walked about 30 miles to Yoas' Agua Caliente Ranch in Amado. The ranch, named for a natural hot springs in the Santa Ritas, was about seven miles east of the Nogales Highway. Yoas ran what was called a rawhide and baling wire outfit, using runaway kids and old derelicts to work his cattle. He picked up most of his help in Tucson at the Ozark Bar on South 6th Avenue, and occasionally at Owl Drug Store or the bar at the Santa Rita Hotel.

Austin had been to the ranch before to visit his older brother, Charlie, who was already living there and knew Yoas needed a good cook. When extra people showed up, Byrd just added water to the beans and made more biscuits. When the beans got sour, Byrd would add a little baking soda and serve them up, producing the inevitable gastrointestinal results. Since Austin had done a lot of cooking at his grandma's, he soon took over the kitchen detail. He even rated the luxury of his own room - a small space converted from a porch off the kitchen.

As the newest hand, one of his jobs was to fill the water troughs early in the morning and to avoid toting the heavy buckets he rigged up a gas pump and engine. Yoas wouldn't let the boys drive his pickup, so the crew used a horse and a 100-pound block and tackle to pull the windmills.

Austin Moss packing the burros with salt at the Yoas Ranch, Dec. 7, 1941. Photo courtesy Austin and Marka Moss.

On one occasion, the crew went to Tucson and bought a 5,000-gallon water tank. It was too big to take on the highway, so they sneaked it to the ranch at night on back roads. Austin stood in the bed of the pickup and propped the electric wires up with a long mesquite pole so they could drive underneath the lines. He said, "If it would have been wet, it would have blown me clear off the truck." He used about $100 worth of pennies patching up the tank once they got it home.

Another of the young boys working for Yoas at the time was Bill Hart, who later married Betty Rae Kane. Yoas sent him to the pasture to set new posts between the existing ones. They planned to pull out the old posts when they got the new fence strung. Bill went to work and busily set all the posts adjacent to the old ones. When Yoas saw what he had done he told him, "You're so sorry Bill, your piss (sic) wouldn't rust a nail." After working from June to September, Austin's total paycheck came to $30.

Austin Moss, Jack Yoas, Charlie Moss and Byrd Yoas at the Yoas Ranch in the 1940s.
Photo courtesy Austin and Marka Moss

Austin has been raising cattle for himself and others ever since, and almost everything he knows about working on a ranch, he learned from the old cowboys at Agua Caliente. One was Ed "Dad" Cunningham, an Irishman and a drunk who Yoas took in after he was blackballed from the railroad.

Another was Pete Cañada, an old bronc rider who stashed bottles of liquor all over the ranch. Despite being half under the weather most of the time, Cañada taught Austin a lot about horses and how to break colts. One day, the crew was assigned to round up horses on the range. Cañada came in with a bad hangover and told Austin to saddle up a jenny mule he had been breaking. The mule was uncooperative, so Austin tied her hard and fast to the hitching post while he struggled with the saddle. Pete looked over at him and said, "You remind me of an old colored guy named Rastus!" From that day, Austin was called Rastus.

Petra Ramirez Lee and her daughter Maria Candida Lee (Moss). Ca 1875.
Photo courtesy Austin Moss.

Moss Family

Austin Moss can trace his family roots to the early days of Arizona's history. His grandfather, who was also named Austin Moss, came to Tucson in 1877 as the blacksmith with a traveling circus. The San Pedro River ran so deep that the performers made the crossing on the backs of the elephants and horses. During the passage, Moss permanently injured the fingers of his right hand when the cable they were using unraveled and broke.

After leaving the circus, he met a well-known pioneer and Tucson miller, James "Jimmy" Lee. Jimmy Lee, born in Ireland in 1833, was instrumental in settling the Oracle area. Lee offered Moss his oldest daughter, Maria Candida, in marriage and gave the couple property beside his gristmill, which later became Eagle Milling Company. Grandfather Austin had his own shop and worked for city parks. He and Maria had eight children and years later Maria would also raise her young grandsons, Austin and John.

Maria Moss, also known as Mary, was a descendant of the Ramírez family that settled in southern Arizona when it was still part of Mexico. Her grandfather, Rafael Ramírez was a soldier stationed at the Presidio de San Augustine in Tucson. Apache raids were so constant that the local citizens sought protection within the walled confines of the Presidio. When provisions ran out, a group of cowboys was sent to the Babacomari Ranch near Elgin to bring back wild cattle to feed the starving people. Rafael rode along as one of their military escort. On May 10, 1848, he was killed when the party rode into an Apache ambush in the

Whetstone Mountains. All 15 were massacred.

Perhaps the most illustrious of the Ramírez clan was Teodoro, the godson and protégé of Father Pedro de Arriquibar, a Franciscan priest who came to Tumacacori in 1775 and later was chaplain in Tucson. The elderly priest taught young Teodoro how to read and write and employed him as his secretary for the last eight years of his life. On his deathbed the priest dictated his Will, leaving all his worldly goods to his 29-year-old godson and his siblings. According to an article by James Officer and Henry Dobyns in "The Journal of Arizona History," Autumn 1984, "The document was signed by the post commander, Lt. Jose Romero and witnessed by Ensign Antonio Comaduran," (as well as four other military officers). "The priest's property included books, livestock, religious artifacts, a house and furniture and nearly 800 pesos."

Austin Moss' great-grandmother Petra Ramirez Lee and grandmother Maria Lee Moss with the Moss children, (from left) Rose, Charlie, Becky, and Jessie. Ca 1898 – 1900.
Photo courtesy Austin Moss

Comaduran later married Theodoro's sister and became Commandante of the Presidio. It was his misfortune to order the military escort, including his nephew Rafael, to their deaths in the Whetstones. By the time of his death at the age of 79, Theodoro was a prosperous businessman, grocer and landowner and had served as justice of the peace in Tucson.

Austin's Grandmother Maria was educated at a convent in Mexico. Austin remembers, "She'd bawl me out in rapid-fire Spanish, so I learned to speak it at an early age. It came in handy after I got married and was hired by the Department of Agriculture for a job in Mexico."

Austin Moss at a picnic at the Babacomari Ranch in Elgin. The brown jug tied to his saddle is filled with gas for the pump. His mount is Red Light, a paint mare owned by Byrd Yoas.
Photo courtesy Austin Moss.

Austin worked at Byrd Yoas' Agua Caliente Ranch for eight years. He supplemented his income by riding young bulls at Kinsley's to see if they would be good for the rodeos that were held there. After one such session, he was pretty banged up and needed a ride home. He asked Monta Carol Gardner (Morgan) if she could give him a lift and she told him she was with the Collie girls, but thought it would be okay. This was the first time he met his future wife, Marka Collie.

Austin and Marka Collie (Moss) standing in front of her parents' home at Mustang Ranch in Elgin shortly before their wedding in 1948. Photo courtesy Marka Moss

After returning from service in WWII he ran into Marka again at a dance. She had come with Bill Brophy, of the Babacomari Ranch, but Bill was into partying and Marka wanted to dance. Austin seized the opportunity and he and Marka danced the night away. They were married June 10, 1948 with Byrd Yoas serving as best man.

The newlyweds worked at the Buenas Aires Ranch for a time, then spent several years in Mexico with the Department of Agriculture on a project to eradicate hoof and mouth disease. The work took him to remote areas where there were no restaurants but local widows could be counted on to provide good meals for a reasonable price. At one such home, Austin ordered ham and eggs. After wash-

Enjoying the races at the Hippodromo de las Americas in Mexico City in 1948. Austin is seated at right rear behind the group of four women. Three of the women's husbands were part of the Dept. of Agriculture project to combat hoof and mouth disease. All three were expecting babies. From left Tommye Kane, Betty Rae Middleton (Hart), Tommye's sister who had come down to help with the expected birth, Monte Joe Kane and Marka Moss. 1948.
Photo courtesy Austin and Marka Moss.

ing up, he wondered why his meal wasn't ready when everyone else had eaten. He noticed a hen sitting on a lariat coiled on the windowsill. The cook waited patiently and eventually the hen laid another egg – Austin's breakfast was ready. "She had a lot of faith in her livestock," Austin said.

After returning to Arizona Austin became foreman at the Swinging H, now the Research Ranch, and helped out at many other outfits in the area. In 1958, Marka's parents, Stone and Fern Collie, gave the young couple 40 acres of land in Elgin. There they built the home where they have lived, reared seven children and raised cattle ever since. He still uses his 1974 Dodge truck to haul cattle but in other ways has adapted to the flow of modern methods. "I started out with a horse and buggy operation," he said, "and just recently, I installed a solar system for my well."

In 1969 Austin hired on with Santa Cruz County as one of only two men handling road construction for the entire county. He retired in 1989 after 20 years of service. "It was one of my better judgment calls. I got a pension, a plaque and a gold watch," he said.

Socorro Jurahui at the age of 24. She loved to attend family dances at the county fair in October and at the Opera House in Patagonia and a dance hall in Harshaw. Music was provided by Alvessa Hummel, Frank Lamma and Jack Turner and his sisters. Photo courtesy Socorro Jurahui.

Socorro Morales Jurahui
Hilario and Porfiria Morales

Seven-year-old Socorro Morales didn't know any English when she started at the Sonoita one-room school. Although she was very shy, she managed to learn the language from listening to the other children in class. When her younger brother George came along, he learned English from her and didn't have as hard a time when he started school.

Socorro remembers that when it rained or snowed the teacher would make them hot chocolate and marshmallows on the wood-burning stove. They had a wind-up phonograph and she would teach the children how to dance to the tune of the "Virginia Reel" and "Put Your Little Foot." Her teacher in fourth grade was Mabel Jean Millett and later she had Miss Young. The school bus driver was Omar Lloyd. She and her lifelong friend, Stayton Brooks, graduated from 8th grade together.

Arizona was still a Territory in 1901 when Socorro's father, Hilario Morales, an orphan at the age of seven, came from Magdalena to live with his aunt and her husband, Severo Miranda in Elgin. The Mirandas lived and worked on the Babacomari Ranch. They treated Hilario as if he was their own son and he always thought of them as his parents.

Hilario began riding and doing chores on the ranch at an early age and later he worked on the railroad under foreman, Charlie Reeves. Socorro's mother, Porfiria Flores, emigrated from Mexico in 1909. She was living with her brother and sister-in-law in Calabasas when she met Hilario. Their first child, Socorro,

Socorro Jurahui's father, Hilario Morales (left) and his uncle, Severo Miranda, in 1915. Hilario was an orphan and came to live with the Mirandas at the Babacomari Ranch in Elgin. They raised him and treated him like their own son.
Photo courtesy Socorro Jurahui.

Porfiria Flores Morales (standing right) was an excellent seamstress and made the outfit she is wearing in this photo. She is pictured with her friend Manuela Echeveria and Manuela's two grandchildren. Ca. 1915.
Photo courtesy Socorro Jurahui.

was born October 14, 1917 in Elgin. Six years later, the little family moved to Sonoita and lived in an adobe house on Reeves' property.

Hilario went to work for Walter Vail on the Empire Ranch. During roundups, he would be gone for weeks at a time, so Socorro and her little brother George, had responsibility for the chores on a daily basis. After school the children carried water from the windmill to the house. They would warm it on the wood stove for their baths, one in the middle of the week and one on Sunday.

Porfiria had earned a living as a seamstress before her marriage and she made all the family's clothes. She had a set routine for the domestic chores. Monday was reserved for washing and starching the clothes. Tuesday she did the sewing and mending and on Wednesdays, she ironed. That left Thursday and Friday for the cleaning.

Many other duties were done on a daily basis. The family had cows, which had to be milked every day, and Porfiria made cheese, butter and cottage cheese. She did all the cooking on a wood stove. They had a window cooler (also known as a desert cooler). It was made from tin and had a piece of wet burlap hanging over it to keep their food refrigerated. Although her father worked for a ranch, they didn't get to slaughter any beef for their own use. Occasionally they would buy beef, but their diet consisted mainly of chicken, eggs, beans, homemade tortillas and produce from their garden.

Porfiria figured out when to plant her garden by the phases of the moon and consulted the almanac on vegetables and flowers. She grew corn, beans, pumpkins and watermelons, all by the dry farming method. Everything that couldn't be eaten right away was dried and saved for winter meals. She hung the squash and chilies on long strings and laid out sliced tomatoes or fruit on a piece of cheesecloth stretched on a board to dry.

Some of Socorro's favorite memories are of the days when her mother would hitch up the one-horse buggy and drive them to Mr. LeGendre's country store in Sonoita. It was a real treat for the children because they would get to buy candy. Socorro especially loved corn flakes, but mother usually bought oatmeal. They would buy Log Cabin syrup in a tin shaped like a real cabin. Her mother saved it for special breakfasts when she would serve it on pancakes topped with lots of homemade butter.

There wasn't much entertainment for children in those days. They had no television, car, phone or electricity and Socorro read by the light of a kerosene lamp. There was no church for them to attend but a minister would come to town for Easter and Mother's Day and hold services at the Sonoita School or the Vaughn Church.

The highlight of the school year was the annual picnic in Hog Canyon every May. All the families would attend. Mr. Heavenor, who worked for Arizona Department of Transportation, requested that day off every year. He loved to sing and he provided the entertainment. Everything was homemade. The mothers cooked for days, preparing fried chicken, potato salad, breads and pies. During the afternoon they would take big chunks of ice, chip it with a hammer and churn it in the freezer to make ice cream. To go with the ice cream, Socorro said Mrs. Heavener made really BIG sugar cookies.

Socorro married Juan Jurahui in 1943. Juan was born in the Rosemont mining area. He did odd jobs and they lived in a small adobe house in Patagonia. Juan died at the early age of 37 leaving her with two young children, Irene and Oscar, to raise by herself. Her parents lived next door and helped her a lot. She worked for the Kolbes at the Rail X Ranch and at the Weatherhead Ranch with Margaret Salge. From 1972 – 1977 she worked as a cook for the Patagonia Grammar School. She made everything from scratch, rolls, pizza, cakes, beans, chicken, tacos, and enchiladas. On Thanksgiving, she and the other cooks fixed a complete turkey dinner with all the trimmings.

Socorro has lived her entire life in the Sonoita and Patagonia area. Her daughter, Irene Smith now lives with her in her home in Patagonia and her niece, Bernie Reindl, daughter of George and Celia Morales, comes by regularly as do her son, granddaughter and three great-grandchildren. Socorro and her old friend Henry Dojoquez both celebrated their 90th birthdays within one month of each other, in the fall of 2007.

FAY ADAMS

One of the Fastest Ropers in the World

Fay Adams was a champion roper
and acted in several silent movies in the 1920s.
Photo courtesy Vera Adams Hunt

Fay Adams

Fay Adams lost both his parents within two days time in 1912. His mother, Domer, died in childbirth. The following day, his father, William, was shot in Colonia Diaz by Pancho Villa's guerillas, leaving their children orphans.

Some of the boys, including Lorin, Fay and Bill, known as "Mexico Bill," eventually ended up on the Arizona side of the border and made their living as cowboys. Along the way, Fay became a championship calf roper, well known on the rodeo circuit. He made an excellent showing at the Tucson Rodeo in 1928 and was touted as the champion calf roper of the world. He worked for ranchers Bud Parker and Roy Adams. Roy was the brother of Ella Braden whose husband, Art, ran the Curley Horse Ranch, but he was not related to Fay.

Fay's brother Lorin worked for the Greene Cattle Company in Cananea and "Mexico Bill," was employed for 30 years at Greene Cattle Company's San Rafael Ranch. Bill carried a sawed off .30 – .30 and a cartridge belt full of ammo. He served on a posse trying to apprehend the pigpen murderers, but when they fled into Mexico he had to give up the chase. It seemed that Bill himself was wanted in that country at the time.

Fay's employer, Bud Parker, also had trouble with Pancho Villa and his revolutionaries. At age 19 Bud went to work for San Domingo Cattle Co. in Chihuahua, Mexico, southwest of Juárez. Several years later, he met Anna Harper, a nurse from San Francisco who was visiting her sister at a neighboring ranch. He and Anna married, and in 1910 she had to flee Chihuahua to escape the fighting. She left on

Lorin Adams, Fay's brother, using a hackamore to break a colt at the Greene Cattle Co. in Cananea, Mexico. Ca. 1915.
Photo courtesy Vera Adams Hunt

Bill Adams, "Mexico Bill," worked for Greene Cattle Company at the San Rafael Ranch for 30 years. He carried a sawed off .30–.30 and a cartridge belt full of ammo and laid his gloves on his horse's neck as he lit up what is probably a hand-rolled cigarette. Ca. 1920s.
Photo courtesy Vera Adams Hunt

a railroad handcar. Villa's men had blown up all the bridges so the handcar had to be towed across many arroyos and creek beds, but she was able to make it safely to El Paso.

Bud Parker stayed on and endured the uprisings until 1916. He sent one of his men to infiltrate Villa's troops to find out when a raid was scheduled. With that information, Parker and his men knew when to drive the mares up into the Sierras for safekeeping. After ten years in Mexico, Bud, along with his brothers, Ope and Dink came to Arizona in 1919, driving a band of horses which they were able to sell for a good price.

Bud became a champion calf and steer roper and a noted breeder and trainer of quality horses. His horses were sought after by cowboys such as Buckshot Sorrells, Tony Altamoreno and Manerd Gaylor. He also supplied roping steers and bucking bulls to rodeo contractors throughout the rodeo west and bought and sold many Sonoran cattle. According to Charlie Fowler, in an article in the Nogales International, Nov. 12, 1986, "He was an exemplary horseman. After a day in the saddle with the cowboys of Sonora both Parker and his horse would be the freshest pair in the group, and Sonora cowboys were some of the best horsemen around."

Fowler also told this story about Bud and his buddy Roy Adams. "We had over 100 head in the corral, waiting to be shipped from the A-7 Ranch near Redington Pass. Bud Parker, the owner was there and said, 'I have given that big, lined-back dun to Roy Adams and he will be here in the morning to pick him up. Adams arrived in a Cord roadster, pulling the first horse trailer I had ever seen. It was made by a blacksmith named Robles who had his shop in Tucson on Main Street at the railroad tracks.

"The trailer had two wheels and was shaped like a big wooden box. The tailgate was secured by two turnbuckles and laid down so a horse could enter. At the front end was an iron ring where the lead rope could be tied. The dun was haltered, and though very nervous, entered the trailer. The tailgate was raised and secured, and the lead rope was tied.

"The dun stood for a few minutes looking around when suddenly he started kicking and lunging. In seconds he had completely destroyed the trailer. All three sides were kicked out and he had dragged the front part, tied to the lead rope, about 300 yards.

He got tangled up in some brush where he stood trembling. Roy looked over his destroyed trailer and said, "Charlie (Fowler), throw your saddle on that dun and take him to my ranch.'"

Fay Adams acted in silent movies in Hollywood in the 1920s. He looked a little like Tom Mix in this photo.
Photo courtesy Vera Adams Hunt, from Fay Adams, Jr. collection.

September 11, 1929 Fay was practicing his roping skills at Bud Parker's ranch north of Nogales in preparation for an upcoming rodeo in El Paso. Two days previously, Adams had finished among winners in the Tubac rodeo. The day after the Tubac event, he made Roy Adams a side bet. The two staged a roping and Fay Adams won. On the second day, as he roped the steer his horse got tangled up in the rope, threw him off and then fell on his head. Dr. Chenowith was called and found that although no bones were broken, Adams had suffered a severe concussion. He died two days later without recovering consciousness. Fay Adams was 31 years old.

The Hummel family in 1917. Back row: Louis G. Hummel, Emma Hummel, son Louis C. Hummel, daughter Villette Donau holding her son Alfred S. Donau II, Son-in-law Alfred S. Donau, daughter Flossie Hummel (Fenter), son Gene Hummel, daughter, Della Hummel (Perry). Front row: son, Don Hummel, son Gail Hummel, granddaughter Aline Donau (daughter of Villette).
Photo courtesy Linda Hummel Roslund

Gene and Alvessa Hummel

Gene Hummel was a 26-year old bachelor when he suddenly found himself in sole charge of running the family's homestead north of Sonoita. Four years previously his parents and youngest siblings had moved to Tucson where his father, Louis G. Hummel set up a law practice. Louis G. had left the running of his Sonoita homestead to four of his older children, Louis C., Flossie, Della and Gene, but circumstances had taken a sudden and dramatic turn.

The two girls got married. Flossie hooked up with Wick Fenter whose pioneer family had arrived in the area in 1870, and Della married Guy Perry, whose mother was Wick's sister. Then Louis C. was drafted into the army in WWI. That left Gene, who was faced with the prospect of handling the remote homestead by himself.

The life was lonely, the work backbreaking and the rewards practically nonexistent. All the proceeds of the operation went to supporting Louis G. and his family in Tucson. When the four youngsters had first been left in charge, Gene tried to continue his education at Tucson High School. The trip to town consumed a day and a half of travel time, meaning that he had to spend a few days there and still try keep up with the chores at the homestead. Combined with the lack of proper clothing and shoes it became too difficult for him to continue. At one point he went to California to learn drafting and was an amateur inventor for the rest of his life, but his formal schooling had come to an abrupt halt.

Gene Hummel behind the plow at the Hummel Ranch. 1920.
Photo courtesy Linda Hummel Roslund

Gene's father, Louis G. Hummel, had been a successful attorney in Cincinnati, with an elegant home in the city and a comfortable summer place in the country. He was reckless in his financial dealings and lost his fortune in 1907 when his investments in a gas company in Benson, Arizona and some mining interests went bankrupt. He left his wife and their new baby, Don, in Ohio and came west with the rest of the children. His oldest child, Villette, was already living in Tucson at that time, with her first husband Percy Seybold.

Louis filed for a homestead in Cortaro, north of Tucson. His wife, Emma, along with her mother, Elizabeth Yockey, and baby, Don, joined them on Christmas Eve, 1907 and the family moved to the Cortaro property. They lived in an old boxcar while they "proved up" the homestead.

Life on the rugged frontier took its toll on Emma. She had lived a pampered lifestyle in Ohio and was suddenly reduced to cooking and baking on a wood stove, doing the laundry on a washboard and raising her own six children plus Aline, Villette's daughter. There was no running water in the house, no electricity and no telephone. She tried to keep up her standards by putting cloth napkins in her children's lunchboxes, but the local children ridiculed them for using what they referred to as "rags."

The Hummel family on an outing at Sweetwater Canyon, in the Gardner Canyon area. Gene Hummel on rock, Don Hummel with gun, Aline Donau, Gail Hummel scaling rock, parents Emma and Louis Hummel standing. Ca. 1917. Photo courtesy Linda Hummel Roslund

As an attorney, Louis G. had represented one of the widows of the owners of the original placer mines in Greaterville, now known as Kentucky Camp. The widow was not interested in the property, so she gave the mine to Louis as payment for his services in representing her in court while she retained other assets of the estate. Louis had a secret desire to mine the property but that never came to pass. His daughter Flossie and her husband Wick Fenter ended up living there and running cattle on it. Eventually a corporation was formed, with each of the children receiving a one seventh interest. When the Fenters didn't take care of the land, let the house fall into disrepair and stopped paying rent, they were evicted, causing an enormous rift in the family.

The Hummel homestead was located at the end of Curley Horse Ranch Road, about 15 miles from the Kentucky Camp property, and was called "The Cottonwoods." A man named Lopez had originally homesteaded there in the early 1900s and built a house behind the old water tank. Legend has it that the gringos tried to take his land and rather than turn it over to them, he hanged himself from one of the cottonwood trees. His body is buried in an unmarked grave on Hummel's property, a mile from the ranch house. Gene piled rocks up on the spot, so that they would always be able to locate the gravesite.

The Hummels started out by dry farming and slowly began adding cattle. When Louis C. returned from the war, he and Gene ran the ranch together. In 1930 Louis C. married Ina Baker from St. David and moved away. From then on Gene ran the ranch by himself. Seven years later he met Alvessa Ochoa at a party at Grace Pomeroy's home in Patagonia. Alvessa and her fellow musicians were holding a jam session and Gene was enthralled. According to their daughter, Linda Hummel (Roslund), " Dad always said he fell in love with her music first and then with her. He loved to dance and was her biggest fan until the day he died," Linda added.

Gene and Alvessa were married in 1937 and moved into the original adobe house on the Hummel homestead built by his father. His youngest brother, Gail, had been born there in 1911. Gene had to purchase the land from his father, although he had been working it and sending the proceeds to Tucson for years. Louis G. also confiscated land from his son, Louis C. in payment of a supposed debt. The adobe house had been built in 1912 and had six rooms and an outhouse, plus a kitchen, saddle room, living room and three other small rooms. Gene and Alvessa added porches, den bedroom and bath in the 1940s.

Gene hired Harold Guyton to build the fireplace and he and Alvessa put in

A picnic was held at "The Cottonwoods" on the Hummel Ranch near Sonoita to plan a Fairgrounds for Santa Cruz County. The Fairgrounds was incorporated in 1915 and has become the heart of community activities in the county. Ca. 1910.
Photo courtesy Linda Hummel Roslund and the Bowman Archives Center

the hardwood floors. He paneled the den and built doors of redwood. Alvessa carved a beam of ivy for the den. She also laid the Spanish tiles in the porches and carved a horse's head on the gate in front of the house.

Alvessa Ochoa was born in Patagonia, one of five children in the family that survived to adulthood. Her father died when she was 17 and she and her brother, Bonafacio "Pacho" Ochoa, supported the family by playing music at dances and Mexican bailes in Harshaw, Lochiel, Washington Camp, Patagonia and Nogales.

Alvessa graduated in the first class that attended all four years in the new school

Alvessa Hummel riding at the Hummel Ranch. Ca 1938.
Photo courtesy Linda Hummel Roslund

in Patagonia. Previously the high school classes had been held in the Patagonia Opera House. One of her teachers was Anna Fortune, who recognized Alvessa's abilities and arranged for her to get a scholarship at Sierra Madre College, now Loma Linda, in Arlington, California. The school was operated by the Seventh Day Adventists and was very strict. Students were not allowed to eat meat and the only music Alvessa could play was hymns. She was used to a more carefree lifestyle and after one year she returned to Patagonia and began teaching Mexican people to speak English and helping them to pass their citizenship tests.

Alvessa and her brother had their own band and played gigs every Saturday night, twelve months of the year. She bought her first saxophone for $15 when

Alvessa Hummel with her band at Cady Hall in Patagonia. From left: Drummer Pops Gregory, Louis Sotomayor from Nogales who was sitting in for fun, Eddie LeGendre on the piano, Alvessa and Pierce (Herb) LeGendre on sax. Ca 1948.
Photo courtesy Linda Hummel Roslund.

she was only 16 and it remained her favorite instrument. Until that time, she had never played one note of music. In the 1940s, she enlisted Ed and Pierce LeGendre, who were in high school at the time, to join the band. They were natural musicians and Alvessa taught them to play the saxophone, drums, piano and trombone. Her band played at the fairgrounds for the rodeo, at family dances on weekends and at the Elgin Club for their parties. It bothered her that Mexican people were not allowed to attend events at the Club and when she was invited, she refused to join.

Alvessa was also an avid amateur archeologist. She knew of places all around the Empire Ranch were there were authentic Indian relics and had permission from the Boice family to hunt for artifacts there. She often took her daughter, Linda, on hikes through the area, searching for treasures and had a wonderful collection of metates, a perfect tomahawk and numerous arrowheads, all from the Hohokam period. Gene was putting in fence posts in front of the house one day when he accidentally broke an ancient skull with his pick. Alvessa glued it together and put it on the mantle, but "she felt guilty and went out and buried it in the rose bushes," Linda said.

Linda remembers rodeo dances at the fairgrounds when the teenagers would go home to change from their Levis into squaw dresses for the dance, which lasted from 9 p.m to 1 a.m. "At 1:00, they would pass around the hat to see how long people wanted the music to continue," Linda said. "They had the Supper Waltz at midnight and women brought tamales, pies and cakes. The band never took a break except for the Supper Waltz. There was no drinking allowed, so people brought their own liquor and spiked the Cokes. In the old pictures, you can see cokes stacked all over the piano."

When Linda was old enough to go to school, the Santa Cruz County School Board came to her parents and asked them to send her to Sonoita School because they didn't have enough children to keep it open. Her parents agreed as long as they agreed to let her stay there and not be transfered to the Empire School when they had enough children to fill the quota.

Mrs. LeGendre was her teacher for the first three years, and she was very strict. "We would have to sit at our desk and put our hands on the table with our fingers showing. She would come with a ruler to see if our hands were clean. If our nails were dirty, we'd get snapped with the ruler. If our hair wasn't combed, we got hit.

"In Mrs. Allen's fourth grade class, there was a fight one day between two kids.

Butchering beef at a Sonoita area ranch. Two cowboys have side of beef hoisted up between tall poles with a pulley in the middle. Ca. 1920s.
Photo courtesy Linda Roslund Hummel.

The teacher split the schoolyard in half. We had the two sides and you couldn't cross the boundary. I picked the side for the playground and to go to the bathroom, you had to get permission to cross the line. Some of the kids I remember from those days were Dorothy and Billie Anna Douglass, the Ambroses, Mary Kellogg, Mercy Jimenez, Sharon and Jokie Spencer, the Cornwalls and Herman Dojoquez."

Jose Urquides, from Greaterville, drove a large van to pick up the high school age ranch children and transport them to Sonoita, where they caught the school bus to Patagonia High School. Linda said this arrangement worked well except for one memorable winter storm when Jose's van got stuck in the snow and they didn't get to Sonoita in time to catch the bus.

When she was about 14, Linda had a crush on a neighbor, Larry Feldman. Larry went to the Baptist Church and he and all the other kids were going to a summer church camp. Linda wanted to attend also, but it was required that each camper attend three Sunday services prior to registration. Linda's family was not religious, but she went every week and was accepted. When she got to camp she discovered that no singing or dancing was allowed. "The camp counselor told me I would rot in Hell because I danced," Linda remembered.

Gene's younger brother, Don, had served as mayor of Tucson in the 1950s and had a lot of influential friends. In the 1960s, General Acceptance Corporation (GAC) put pressure on Don to persuade Gene and Alvessa to sell the ranch. GAC had purchased the adjoining Empire Ranch and wanted the Hummel property also. Don Hummel negotiated an agreement whereby, as a condition of the sale, GAC would also purchase the 3200 deeded acres at Greaterville.

The Hummels retained a life estate on the property and lived there until they passed away, Gene in 1974 and Alvessa in 1982. The property was later sold to Anamax Mining Co. and is now, along with the Empire Ranch, part of the Las Cienega National Conservation Area. It is managed by the Bureau of Land Management.

The town of Greaterville as it looked in 1894.
Photo courtesy of the Bowman Archives Center

Greaterville and Kentucky Camp

The date was April 15, 1915. A crime had been reported in Greaterville. Sheriff Albert. W. Forbes sent two deputies to the area to investigate the disappearance of Loretta Yanez, who had a goat ranch nearby. Witnesses told Deputies Robert Fenter and Frank Moore that Antonio Encinas has probably murdered the woman.

Moore and Fenter went to the home of the Leon brothers, and charged Hilario, Jose Maria and Francisco Leon with refusing to disclose the whereabouts of their brother-in-law, Alberto Encinas. They tied the hands of the three suspects and strung them up on a branch of what is now known as the "Hanging Tree," reportedly to make them talk. Hilario Leon, 19 years old, died at the scene of the hanging, Jose Maria died two weeks later of spinal meningitis and Francisco escaped into the hills.

Fenter and Moore were tried for murder in Pima County Superior Court, June 26, 1919. According to court records, "The defendants admitted that they strung up and 'stretched' the three Leon brothers one at a time in order to elicit information as to the whereabouts of Antonio Encinas. They indicated they did this two or three times on each of the brothers and when they passed out and fell down they waited until they revived and continued the process."

The brothers turned out to be innocent of any wrongdoing and the murderer was never apprehended. The deputies were convicted of second-degree murder and sentenced to ten years to life in prison. The "Hanging Tree" still stands north of Greaterville.

In the late 1800s, the area originally known as the Santa Rita Mining District was a thriving community with a post office, school, dance halls, saloons and stores. Alvah Smith was the first to discover gold in the hills when he prospected there in 1874. Word spread rapidly and by June of 1875 approximately 400 miners were living there in tents and huts dug into the hillsides.

The name was officially changed from Santa Rita to Greaterville, after a man named Greater, when the Post Office was established January 3, 1879. The first Postmaster was Thomas Steele.

Placer mines ranged across the hills in a large area that included the townsite and what is now referred to as Kentucky Camp. Over the next ten years about $500,000 worth of gold would be taken out of the area, with the largest nugget said to weigh 37 ounces, worth about $630.

Legend has it that when the Mexican miners put on a *baile*, cowboys would come from the nearby Empire Ranch. One night, the miners decided they didn't want to share their girls with the cowboys, locked the door to the dance hall and refused to let them in. The cowboys noticed smoke coming from the chimney and one of them climbed on the roof and dropped in a handful of live cartridges. The shells went off with a huge bang, miners poured out the door in a panic and the cowboys grabbed the señoritas and proceeded to the dance floor. Tempers flared but there were no injuries. Afterwards, the owners of the Empire invited the miners and their families to be their guests at the ranch.

Water was scarce and was brought in canvas sacks on the backs of burros from Gardner Canyon, several miles away, and sold for .03 cents a gallon. Lack of water combined with Apache raids and dwindling gold discoveries led to the area's demise in the late 1880s. A brief resurgence occurred when James Stetson, a mining engineer, got the idea to pipe seasonal runoff from nearby streams into a reservoir that would hold enough water to last for ten months.

He persuaded a wealthy businessman, George McAneny to invest in the Santa Rita Water and Mining Co. and they built a headquarters near the Greaterville townsite, in Kentucky Gulch. Stetson fell from a window of the Santa Rita Hotel in Tucson in 1904, a possible suicide. McAneny died five years later. McAneny's heirs did not want the property and turned the title over to Louis G. Hummel, the attorney representing the estate, in exchange for his services.

One of the first white men to come to Greaterville back in its glory days was Tom Hughes. Donald Honnas, whose mother delivered the mail to Greaterville three days a week, tells of an incident that happened in 1910: "Joe Pallanes and a friend wanted to put on a dance and Mr. Hughes' house was the only place large enough. Hughes agreed that he would move everything out and they could have the dance there. When the two left, Hughes was standing at the door. The boys were on their way to arrange for the music when they were overtaken on the road and told that Hughes had been struck and killed in his doorway by a lightning bolt."

Dixie Collie was one of the teachers at the one-room Greaterville School. There was no place for her to board, so her brother Bill Collie, went to Nogales and bought lumber to construct a one-room shack near Mr. Pfiffer's store. Late one night Dixie was awakened by someone trying to force open her door. She grabbed a pistol her brother had provided her and when the person continued pounding, all the while mumbling incoherently, she pointed toward the door and pulled the trigger.

Dixie had shot Mr. Pfiffer, the drunk storekeeper, who had mistaken her house for the outhouse. "I shot him in the side, low down, but the bullet pierced his lung and came out his back. Fortunately, there were two or three men at the store playing poker and they took him to Tucson for a doctor." Although Dixie's memoirs indicate that Mr. Pfiffer recovered from his wounds, most accounts of the day say he did not survive. He is reported to have avowed on his deathbed that the shooting was his own fault. He had warned the teacher to never let anyone in the door after dark.

The Post Office closed its doors in 1946. Only a few families remained in the area. Eventually the school closed, the desks and blackboards were moved to the nearby Empire School and the remaining students transferred there also.

In the 1930s Louis G. Hummel's heirs formed a corporation for the ownership of the Greaterville property. General Acceptance Corporation (GAC) purchased the Empire Ranch in the 1960s hoping to use their water to develop the Rosemont Mine in the north end of the Santa Ritas, and wanted the adjacent Hummel homestead property owned by Gene and Alvessa Hummel.

Gene's younger brother, Don, a past mayor of Tucson, negotiated an agreement whereby, as a condition of the sale of the Hummel homestead, GAC would also purchase the 3,200 deeded acres at Greaterville. Jose and Angelita Urquides, who had lived in the Greaterville townsite for many years, filed a successful claim for 80 acres of land citing as legal precedent the rule of Adverse Possession.

According to an article in the Tucson Daily Citizen, February 28, 1974, Anamax Mining Co. purchased the 3,140-acre property from GAC for $1.2 million. It was later sold to a developer who exchanged it with the Forest Service for property elsewhere.

The United States Forest Service began restoration work on the McAneny buildings in 1991 with the help of a volunteer group of interested people and renamed the property Kentucky Camp.

Cora Everhart taught in rural schools across the county for 30 years and served as Santa Cruz County Superintendent of Schools from 1942 to 1965.
Photo courtesy Bowman Archives Center

Cora Everhart

The only thing they feared was Hell-fire or ending up in the "Poorhouse." To Cora Everhart's parents, those were the real fears. The everyday hardships of life were simply challenges to be overcome or endured. Hardships they had aplenty, but Cora, who was born in Iowa in 1883, said that her mother made sure her children went to church every Sunday and never wasted anything that could be put to good use.

"The Poorhouse was a very real thing, just over the hill. My mother often mentioned it to me when I was wasteful of food. I never saw the Poorhouse. I made sure I never would, by working, saving and getting the education available," Cora explained in her memoirs.

Her father was typical of the pioneers of the era, moving every few years, chasing his dream of forging a new life on the frontier. The family left Iowa and lived in a variety of small communities and mining camps across Kansas, Colorado, and Texas.

The woman who was destined to become an icon in the small community of Elgin in southeast Arizona, and a respected teacher and Superintendent of Schools for Santa Cruz County, was often in danger of failing to get a proper education. Due to their migratory lifestyle, Cora was 16 before she graduated from 8th grade and had to take extra classes to graduate from high school so she could qualify for a teaching certificate.

At the age of five she walked half a mile to school in Kansas, where about 40 students, ranging in age from five to 21, were crammed into one small classroom. There were about 18 "first readers," who were told to open their books and study the lesson, with no further instruction. Cora said, "All I knew was to drop my eyes and open my book, at which I stared. When called upon (none of us) could read. Our punishment was to stand in line toeing a mark. I remember my legs aching."

The first graders were crowded together, three to each double seat meant for two, and invented ways to look busy. "We stood our books on end, spreading the leaves and pretending it was a horse.

"Water was carried in a bucket from a neighbor's well about one-half mile away.

Two boys chosen for this chore considered it a favor, and gladly brought a full bucket. It was passed up and down the aisles, each child drinking from the same dipper.

"I remember watching a small boy who sat behind me using a straw to chase a louse up and down his pencil groove. The weekly tub bath included a kerosene, or coal oil, shampoo and a fine tooth combing."

Once Cora graduated, she lost no time in looking for work. She accepted a teaching position at a one-room school in Caddoa, a small Colorado town. Arriving at the school, Cora wondered why a high fence surrounded the building. The enclosed area was much too small for a playground. The mystery was solved when she learned that a wild bull had charged the children and previous teacher on the unfenced playground. The children rushed through the open door and the teacher climbed through the window. The fence was speedily erected, but the teacher applied for a position elsewhere.

Her landlady, "Grandma" Barker took Cora aside one day and gave her this piece of advice: "Never welcome the attentions of a young man of poor financial prospects." Cora said, "I met the man of good moral character and more than good financial prospects. He asked me to marry him. It was too late. I had already met the young man of poor financial prospects. We celebrated our Golden Wedding Anniversary October 26, 1956."

Charles Everhart turned serious at the prospect of marriage and took a job as a fireman with the Union Pacific Railroad. The couple moved to Rawlins, Wyoming where Charles was on call duty, putting in long hours shoveling coal. After three years Charles was promoted to locomotive engineer, paid in script that was only accepted at one store, and endured violent strikes as labor unions became more aggressive.

Cora's father had recently bought a farm in Texas. He needed help and offered Charles and Cora 40 acres of tillable land. Charles accepted, resigned his job, and they set to work plowing, planting cotton and building a one-room house. They soon ran out of money and Charles looked for railroad work while Cora applied to again teach school.

Front porch of the Everhart's home in Rock Springs, Wyoming. (From left) A neighbor woman, Cora's sister Dora and her three children, Cora Everhart. Ca. 1907.
Photo courtesy Sharon Everhart Perrill

Charles headed west, walking, riding or hitchhiking and picking up work along the way. When he reached Tucson, he was hired on as a switch engineer in the Southern Pacific Railroad yard. Charles blew the train whistle February 14, 1912, when Arizona Territory became the 48th state. Cora said, "I heard Tucson city bells ring; my husband tooted a switch engine whistle and all the city celebrated Arizona's first birthday.

Cora got her Arizona teaching certificate and soon landed a job in a one-room school in Mammoth. As in Caddoa, the previous teacher had left abruptly. According to local reports, "she fled in a panic," and no classes had been held for several weeks. "When I landed there, after traveling nearly all day by stage, I found I was expected to live under the most primitive conditions in the old unused school building. The only stove was an old wood heater set in the center of the barn-like room. Nearby were a cot and the bedding where the former teacher had slept. A pile of stove wood near the door and a bucket for carrying water from a neighbor's pump completed the preparation for the teacher.

"Crawling into the used bedding, I caught the skin disease which caused my predecessor to panic and leave. A doctor gave me an ointment and advised me to take a soapy bath and anoint each spot twice a day, a shivering cure in mid-winter. My bathroom was a spot near the stove, sheltered by coats draped on backs of chairs. Little did I realize when I signed their contract that I would request a release a month or so later."

Meanwhile, Charles had filed for a 160-acre homestead nine miles southwest of Elgin. At first they lived in two tents, which they later converted into tent houses. They installed floors, windows, doors and a roof. "The Home Comfort range was my pride and joy. Not many stoves had a warming oven and a hot water reservoir. What food we had! Great flaky delicately browned loaves of bread, pots of beans cooked with home cured salt pork seasoned with chili. And the gingerbread made from Will Collie's homemade sorghum," Cora said.

When the Everharts moved onto the property there had been no rain since the winter snows. The shallow natural depressions were going dry and "wild cattle were bogging

The homestead that Cora and Charles built nine miles southeast of Sonoita. Pre-1920.
Photo courtesy Sharon Everhart Perrill

down in the mud trying to get the last swallow of muddy water," Cora remembered. Neighbors offered them well water and they hauled about five barrels each time. Feeling they were imposing, they planned to drill their own well. They were advised that the water level was far from the surface, but they struck water at 118 feet. Cora told Charles, "I am teaching. I can pay for the drilling, and a windmill." She added, "With an olla full of water hanging in the shade under a tree, we had plenty of cool drinking water. California Coolers, wooden frames of shelves wrapped in canvas under a drip in a shady porch, kept our food cool, our milk sweet."

"My grandparents made a cute couple," Sharon Perrill said. Charles was 6' tall and Cora was a tiny 5' powerhouse. She wasn't afraid of anything. One day she went outside with her egg basket, dressed in her nightgown and slippers. A large calf playfully knocked her down. The next day she was ready for him. When he bounded up she "cold cocked" him with a two by four she had left by the door. He didn't bother her again." Cora had a real affinity for nature and told Sharon, "When I die, I want to come back as a chicken, so I can scratch in the earth all day."

One afternoon during the spring drought, Cora and Charles had eaten their dinner and spread out a blanket in the cool shade of a large oak tree for a siesta. They could see the Patagonia Trail about five miles away and spotted smoke rising up in the clear air. "Luckily, my husband had hauled a load of water, the wagon was loaded, the barrels mostly full. Horses were rounded up and harnessed, ready to go as near as possible to the fire line.

"Volunteer firemen began arriving by horseback or in wagons. The forest ranger came with a wagon of water and organized the group. From the tiny spot the fire spread, burning a range about five miles long till it surrounded a peak just behind our house. At last the fire line was stabilized. With a great roar the fire rushed to the top, leaving a few stumps to burn to ashes.

"Black, grimy and dirty, they had fought two days and nights with no sleep except a few hours at night on a blanket out of doors. Now they were going home, happy and content with the cash money they received. I was grateful for the .35 cents I received per meal."

In 1915 Cora began her second year teaching in the Vaughn district. She had bought a gentle mare, Black Bess, from the Royal Bakery in Tucson when they converted to motor delivery. She hitched Bess to a topless buggy for the ride to school and the horse stopped at every gate as if she were delivering a loaf of bread. Cora took off a few weeks for the birth of her son, Jack, then hired a neighbor, Mrs. Jolly, to care for him when she went back to teaching. When Jack was about two,

Cora and Charles Everhart on a "well-used" wagon at their homestead.
Photo courtesy Sharon Everhart Perrill

Cora's crippled ten-year-old orphan sister came to live with them. .

She gave up her teaching position when she found out that her appointment had been controversial. Needing employment, she took the examination for postmaster and was named Elgin Postmaster, April 19, 1919. She kept Black Bess in an enclosure nearby and hitched her up on Saturdays to drive the children to the ranch where Charles bached it during the week.

Her schedule was onerous with two children to care for, one a baby and the other lame from polio. There was no running water, just a hand pump and bucket across the street. "Relief was on the way. Another sister married and moved to Tucson. She came and took our sister to live with her," Cora said.

Mail traveled from Nogales to Benson and returned once each weekday. Besides the postmaster, two contract carriers delivered the mail to Rain Valley and Canille

Cora Everhart was principal at the two-room Potrero School in the mid-1920s.
Photo courtesy Sharon Everhart Perrill

(Canelo). Elgin was considered a Fourth Class office and the salary was far from adequate, averaging $35 per month, excepting December, when a $10 bonus was paid.

Their tent house had been replaced by erecting adobe walls, iron roof, door and windows, but the interior was a vast open space. They needed to generate more income to cover expenses, so after five years, Cora left the Post Office and applied for a position with the school district. In late August, 1924 Cora and her son, Jack, moved into an apartment in Nogales and she became principal at the Potrero two-room school. Charles resumed baching at the ranch. She spent four years at Potrero and from 1928 to 1942 she taught closer to home, at Elgin, Vaughn and Canille.

Cora was elected secretary of the Santa Cruz County Fair & Rodeo Association in 1932, where she served with distinction for seven years. She tendered a letter of resignation after four years of service to free up some time for study, but President Harold B. Thurber declined to accept. Thurber replied, "Your knowledge of Fair business is needed as the Association prepares to reorganize and I urge you to stay on a while longer." She agreed to continue until the legal incorporation of the Association was finalized.

In 1942, Cora was appointed to fill Mrs. Lulu B. Larimore's un-expired term as Superintendent of Schools. She worked hard to learn the job in the six months left of Larimore's term and then ran for the office. The only time she was opposed was in her first run for office. After her election, Cora attended classes at the University of Arizona and earned her college degree. According to her granddaughter, Sharon Perrill, "She was more proud of that degree than any of her other many accomplishments." Cora Everhart served 22 years, six months, and 16 days as Santa Cruz County School Superintendent, retiring January 1, 1965.

In 1958 Cora sold the homestead property to the Baker family. She remained active and interested in the world around her until her death in January, 1980 at the age of 97.

Pimeria Alta Historical Society
P.O. Box 993
Nogales, Arizona
April 26, 1963

Mrs. Cora Everhart
1119 Morley Ave.
Nogales, Arizona

I am pleased to pass you herewith a Certificate of Honorary Life membership in this Society, as authorized by unanimous vote of the Society at last night's meeting.

Knowing your record of past service to your fellow members and our citizenry at large, I realize this gesture is less than adequate to cancel our obligation.

We look forward in pleasant anticipation of continued close association and cooperation in carrying out the aims and objectives of the P.A.H. Society.

Cordially yours,

W. J. Macgregor

W. J. Macgregor, Secy.

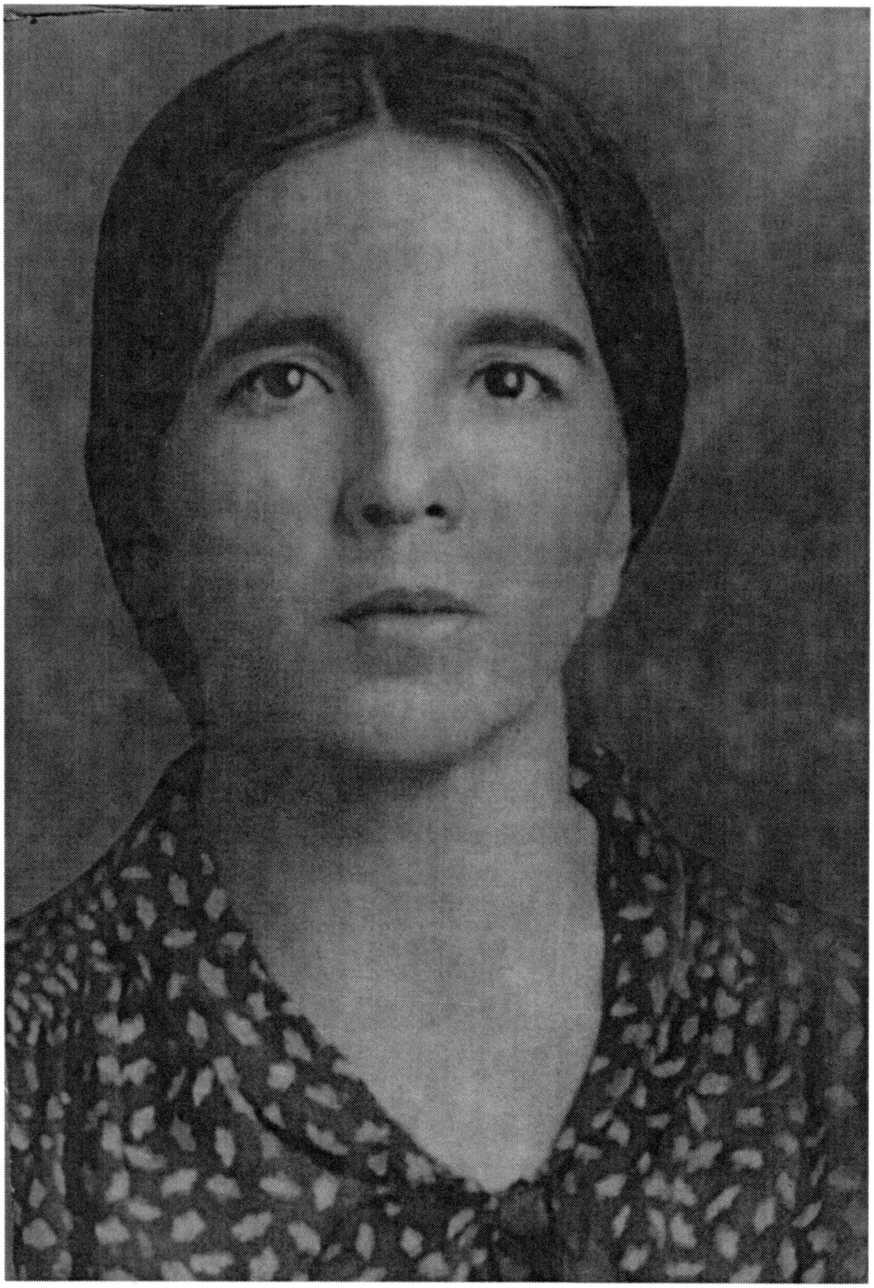

Maria Cruz, "Crucita," Valenzuela as a young woman. Ca. 1914.
Photo courtesy Lupita Ronquillo Santillan

Maria Cruz Valenzuela
Eglantina Ronquillo Mendoza

Lupita Santillan says that her grandmother, a beautiful young village girl from Canelas, Durango, stole the heart of a dashing young engineer who worked for Southern Pacific Railroad. Maria Cruz Valenzuela married Frederico Mendoza in 1916. Maria, known as Cruz or Crucita, wanted to name her firstborn Eglantina, after a beautiful white flower that she discovered in a wash, but her family protested that it was not a saint's name. The resourceful Cruz added several saint's names and the child was christened Maria Eglantina Isabel de la Candelaria Valenzuela Mendoza.

Cruz set out for Culiacán in 1917 to register Eglantina's birth, but raiding bands of Federales were roaming the area. The Federales often kidnapped the young boys for their army and raped the girls. Once a solider had raped a girl, she became his "guacha," and would follow him on foot while he rode horseback. She would be responsible for cooking his meals and washing his clothes. To protect the pretty young girls from the soldiers, the frightened villagers of Canelas put black coal on their faces, tangled their hair and covered their heads with a rebozo (scarf). Thus transformed into haggard old women, the girls would ride a burro out of town, unnoticed by the marauding Federales. They would hide deep in the hills in Sierra Durango until danger had passed.

Cruz's sister, Refugia, was married to a Mexican general, but she had boldly taken a stand on the opposite side of the political fence. Refugia had a boarding house in Cananea and ran a dining room where she served simple meals of soup

Maria Cruz, "Crucita," Valenzuela "a la edad quince anos," at fifteen years of age, while she still lived in Canelas, Durango.Ca. 1910
Photo courtesy Lupita Ronquillo Santillan

and tortillas. Behind this deceptively innocent operation she was engaged in a dangerous collaboration with Pancho Villa and his revolutionaries. Cruz and her two daughters, Eglantina and Rebecca, moved to Cananea to live with Refugia in the early 1920s.

Rebeca Mendoza was born in 1918. She was one year younger than her sister Eglantina. Ca. 1934.
Photo courtesy Lupita Ronquillo Santillan

One of Villa's guerillas was a man called Tortuga, who had contacts in Nogales. He enlisted the aid of Panchita, a prostitute from Canal Street, to help him in a clandestine smuggling operation. There were no fences at that time and it was a simple matter to cross the border at will. Panchita, and later several more girls, were pressed into service to walk across to the Arizona side wearing wide skirts, go to the appointed rendezvous and take delivery of the contraband rifles. They would crack the rifles in half and strap one half to each leg, where they would be completely hidden under their voluminous skirts. Ammo belts were concealed under their jacket or shawl. Once safely back on the Mexican side the girls turned the weapons over to Tortuga, who arranged for them to be delivered to Refugia's boarding house in Cananea.

Refugia had a secret compartment behind the walls of the dining room where she stored the smuggled rifles until Pancho Villa and his men came for them. One day someone tipped off the Federales, who made a raid on the boarding house and discovered the contraband. On the day of the raid, Cruz was bedridden in the back room suffering from an infection in her leg. Eglantina and her sister, Rebecca, were terrified and huddled close by their mother's bed. Years later Eglantina remembered how rough and dirty the men were with their long beards and big sombreros and how they scared her. Even so, they showed a little kindness by dropping some coins on the bedside table for her mother.

Refugia did not get off so easily. The Federales dragged her off and threw her in the local jail, a notorious place known as Cárcel de Cananea. When the General heard about the raid and learned that his wife was incarcerated, he hurried to Cananea and, by bribes or other means, secured her release. He then lost no time in moving Refugia, along with Cruz and her two daughters to Nogales, Sonora, where they would be out of the reach of the opposing sides. The General subsequently deserted the Federales to join Pancho Villa's guerillas and was killed in battle.

During their escape to Nogales, Crucita and Refugia traveled under the name Valenzuela to avoid discovery by the Federales. Once in Nogales, Crucita changed back to her married name of Mendoza. Her children's papers listed that name and that was the only way that she could get them enrolled in school. They lived two blocks from the international border on Arispe Street, the main street in Nogales, now called Avenida Obregón. They lived next door to El Jardín, a fancy nightclub with beautiful hardwood floors and palm trees. Refugia, called "Tia Cuca," by her nieces," raised roses, chickens and ducks that she supplied to the nightclub.

Postcard taken during the Carnival held in Nogales, Sonora, the night before Lent began, similar to the Mardi Gras celebration in New Orleans. Eglantina and her sister, Rebeca, are in costume for the festivities, which were later banned by the Catholic bishop because he felt that the masked people became too uninhibited and did not behave in a Christian manner. Ca. early 1920s.
Photo courtesy Lupita Ronquillo Santillan

In the early 1930s, a young man named Fernando Miguel Ronquillo rode his bicycle back and forth across the border delivering prescriptions to his father's customers. His father, Miguel Fernando Ronquillo, owned a pharmacy on the American side, on the corner of Elm and Arroyo Boulevard. As young Fernando was pedaling through town one day, he was captivated by the sight of a señorita with long black hair that reached halfway down her back. It was Eglantina, who by this time had grown into a beautiful young woman. He liked to pull her hair and she would call him, *Negrito Sambillo*, (Little Black Sambo) because his skin was so dark. She also teased him with *Chango Angorotano*, meaning big, hairy ape.

Ronquillo was an American citizen and wanted Eglantina to become a citizen before they got married. The Ronquillo's' lawyer was Mr. Hathaway, and through him Eglantina was sent to Jim Hathaway's ranch in Parker Canyon for three weeks to establish the residency required to get her papers.

According to their daughter, Lupita Santillan, "I have a brother, Miguel Fernando Ronquillo, II, whose name was a progression in the family tree. Our

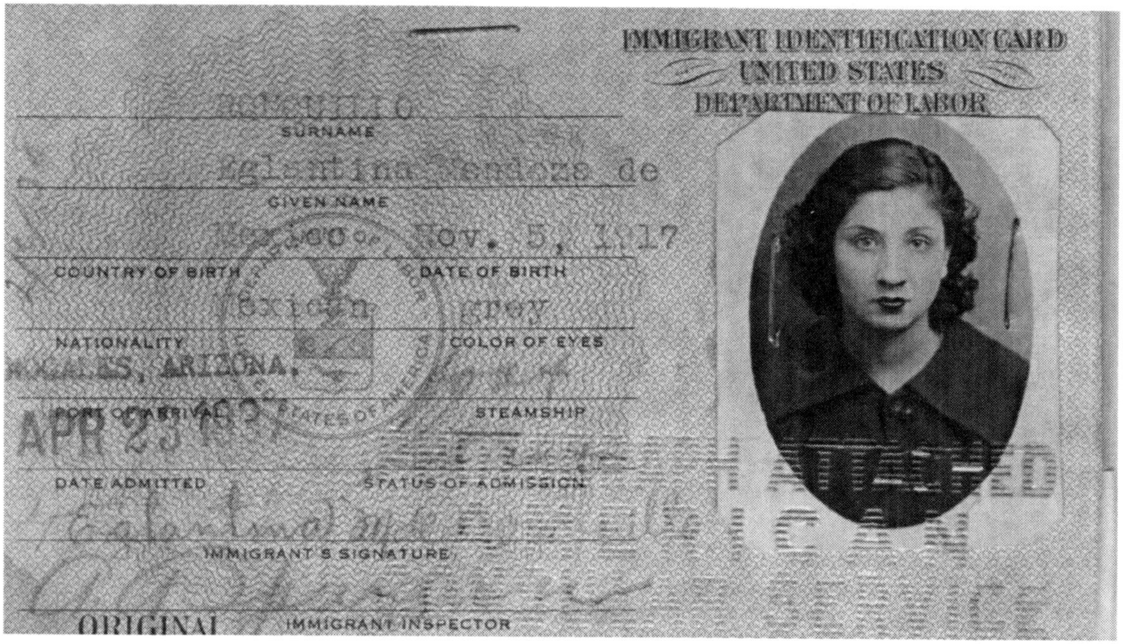
IMMIGRANT IDENTIFICATION CARD
UNITED STATES
DEPARTMENT OF LABOR

SURNAME

GIVEN NAME

Nov. 5, 1917

COUNTRY OF BIRTH — DATE OF BIRTH

grey

NATIONALITY — COLOR OF EYES

ARIZONA.

PORT OF ARRIVAL — STEAMSHIP

APR 23

DATE ADMITTED — STATUS OF ADMISSION

IMMIGRANT'S SIGNATURE

ORIGINAL — IMMIGRANT INSPECTOR

Immigration identification card for Eglantina Mendoza de Ronquillo, dated April 23, 1937. Document courtesy Lupita Ronquillo Santillan

grandfather was Miguel Fernando, my father was Fernando Miguel, my brother was Miguel Fernando, II, and my half brother was Fernando Miguel, Jr." All the women in the family were named Maria. "My grandmother was Maria Cruz (Crucita), and her sisters were Maria de las Angeles, Maria de Refugia (Tia Cuca) and Maria Nieves.

Five-year-old Lupita and her six-year-old brother, Miguel at the old Placita in Nogales, Sonora. Ca. 1943.
Photo courtesy Lupita Ronquillo Santillan

Lupita and her brother were born in Nogales, Arizona in the basement of the Ronquillos' home on Elm Street. Dr. Chenowith delivered Miguel, but Lupita's birth came so fast that there was only time to get a Salvation Army nurse to act as midwife.

Their parents' marriage was not a happy one. "My father was a ladies' man and had many wives and girlfriends. Miguel and I have two half-brothers and a half-sister, " Lupita said. By the time Lupita was three years old, her mother divorced Ronquillo and moved back to Sonora to live with her mother, Cruz.

Fernando and Raul Ronquillo at the Potrero Ranch, north of Nogales, during a snowfall in the winter of 1916. Fernando married Eglantina in the mid-1930s. Fernando's father was a foreman for the ranch owner, Pete Kitchen. Ronquillo and Kitchen were married to sisters from Hermosillo. Ca. 1916.
Photo courtesy Lupita Ronquillo Santillan

Eglantina wanted Lupita and Miguel to go to school in Arizona since they were U.S. citizens. She obtained a job as a nanny for the William Corcoran family in Nogales, Arizona. She and her children moved into the Corcoran's elegant white home near Walter Holm's warehouse, where the Nogales City Hall is now located. The living room had thick white rugs and the house boasted the first swimming pool in Nogales. It took five days to fill the pool.

William and Gertrude Corcoran and their daughter Trudy at their home in Nogales. Ca. mid-1940s. Photo courtesy Lupita Ronquillo Santillan

Corcoran was a produce importer. He and his wife often traveled to Boston where his sister played in the Boston Symphony Orchestra. William was also an accomplished pianist and he played "Rhapsody" and other tunes every afternoon, promptly at 5 p.m. Lupita and her brother were treated like members of the family. They ate and played with Gertrude, "Trudy," the Corcoran's only child. William

Corcoran was later killed in Mexico, piloting his private plane.

One of Lupita's earliest memories is hearing the clinking of the milk bottles delivered by the milkman from the Monte Carlo Dairy. He would leave the fresh milk early in the morning and pick up the empties at 5 p.m. Customers could write a note to the delivery man to order cottage cheese or butter, curl it up inside the neck of the empty milk bottle and he would deliver the order the next morning.

When Lupita grew up and married, she moved to Guadalajara with her new husband, where their little family was involved in a serious auto accident. Lupita was badly injured, and her husband and four-month old baby were killed. Grief-

Maria, "Crucita," Mendoza blessing Julia and Miguel Fernando Ronquillo, II, on their wedding day. Sept. 20, 1969
Photo courtesy Lupita Ronquillo Santillan

stricken, she returned to Nogales to live with her mother and never remarried. She worked for 32 years for Capin's Mercantile Corporation and for ten years at Pennys' in the customer relations department.

A lifelong resident of Ambos Nogales, Lupita lives in an apartment in the old Wise home, built in 1894 and now owned by Hector Castro, Jr. and his mother Socorro. The house was the site of a 24-hour battle on historic Crawford Street during the Mexican Revolution. An old man, Joseph (Papa) Wise, was sitting in the corner of the large living room in what was called the grandfather's chair. A shot came through the front window narrowly missing him, but leaving a permanent bullet hole in the chair.

Lupita and her mother shared an abiding interest in the history of the Pimeria Alta region of northern Sonora and southeastern Arizona. She has three scrapbooks packed with photos, news clippings and magazine articles about the history of the area. Eglantina started the collection in the 1950s, and Lupita adds to it constantly, as she continues to collect historical information and memorabilia.

Lupita Santillan keeps her mother's scrapbooking tradition alive by regularly adding historic photos and newspaper articles.
Betty Barr photo

The Cause

By Sister Mary

Because I have received kindness, I have been spurred to be kind.
Because I have caught a smile on another's lips, I have found myself smiling.
Because I have known the joy of receiving, I rejoice in giving.
Because I have felt pain, I know what pity is.
Because I have tasted humiliation, I know what consideration is.
Because I have seen Christ suffer, I have the courage to go on.

This prayer was sent to Lupita Ronquillo Santillan by a friend, and she credits it as her daily inspiration to move forward and work with people in a giving, loving and productive manner, in spite of the many hardships, losses and rejections she has endured in her lifetime.

Alberto Joffroy wearing his signature straw skimmer as he and his wife, Elinora, enjoy a family picnic. Ca. late 1970s.
Photo courtesy Suzanna Chernin

Alberto Joffroy

Alberto M. Joffroy, a successful Nogales merchant of the last century, cut a jaunty figure as he strolled the downtown streets sporting his signature straw skimmer. His daughters remember that the self-proclaimed "playboy" was seldom seen outside bareheaded, and his large collection of hats included different ones for every season. Another trademark, one with less happy memories, was a crippled right hand, courtesy of a Yaqui Indian raiding party.

It was a cold day in December 1917 when the 26-year-old Alberto got a message from the Governor of Sinaloa that he needed to see him. Although his future father-in-law cautioned him that the trip was too dangerous, Alberto, who at that time was supplying provisions to the Southern Pacific Railroad, decided to risk it. He also offered to serve as an escort to a young woman who was on her way to Culiacán to be married.

The two young people boarded the train in Nogales. After an hour's ride, the 18-year-old girl felt dizzy. Alberto took her out on the caboose to get a breath of fresh air. Suddenly a group of 500 Yaquis surrounded the train and started shooting.

The Mexican government had tried to force the Yaquis to make peace by capturing their women, taking them from their homes in the mountains and sequestering them in Hermosillo. The ploy failed miserably. Rather than make peace, the Yaquis retaliated by derailing the train. Over 60 people were killed and many others were wounded.

The young bride-to-be was shot in the leg, then pulled from the train and fatally stabbed in the chest. Alberto was shot three times. A bullet ripped through his knee and another tore his hand where he was gripping the railing, leaving three fingers dangling by a thread. The Indians dragged him off the train, smashing his face against the railing and scraping him facedown across the cinders. They stripped him of his clothes, shot him once more and left him for dead on the embankment.

A supervisor for Southern Pacific of Mexico came out to the scene and recognized the barely-breathing Alberto. He ordered the brakeman to transport the badly injured young man to the hospital in his private car. Alberto was hospitalized for months because the wound in his arm stubbornly refused to heal. One of his sisters came from Nogales to stay with him throughout the long cold winter. Finally, on April 1, he was well enough to be moved to Nogales, where he spent another month recuperating in bed.

The wounds continued to plague him for the rest of his life, but he overcame the pain and took great pride in demonstrating that he could lift a heavy suitcase with his right hand that only had a thumb and index finger.

Alberto's grandfather, Lorenzo Joffroy, migrated to Sonora from Paris, France. He married a Mexican woman who was related to DeAnza, and they raised their family in the capital of Sonora. Their son, Luis, came to the United States in the late 1870s. He entered the country west of Lochiel and had a store there. In 1881 he moved his family to Nogales, Arizona, where his son Alberto, the ninth of ten children, was born ten years later.

Even as a little boy, Alberto had a sharp eye for business. One of his first purchases was a huge cache of 5,000 marbles that he bought for $2. He sold them for a penny each and then challenged the new owners to a game, whereupon he would win back his inventory and start over again.

The five Joffroy brothers put on a neighborhood circus and charged kids a few pennies to attend. His older brothers were the trapeze artists. Alberto's nickname was "Payaso," because he played the part of a clown. He also manned the entrance and collected the money. Another one of his creative enterprises was making cigarettes out of what he referred to as "horse shit."

By the age of 15 he already had a little shack where he sold Christmas items. He was in the eighth grade. A few years later he went to Empalme to work for the Southern Pacific Railroad. He worked at night as a coal boy and was later promoted to days. He was employed there from 1906 – 1909.

Alberto traveled to California to attend business school in Los Angeles. They offered him a diploma for $10, but he wanted to take the classes and learn everything he could. He worked his way through school with a job at the Santa Fe Railroad. It cost him $25 a month for a hotel room that included breakfast and dinner, and he ate lunch at Fred Harvey's Café, where the workers got a jug of beer and all they could eat for five cents.

Children gathered for a group picture at a fiesta on the Mexican side of the international border at Nogales in front of Dr. Purdy's office. 1899.
Photo courtesy Suzanna Joffroy Chernin.

He bought shoes for $3, a suit for $15, and his first straw skimmer for $1.50.

So began the saga of a sometimes brilliant, sometimes disastrous, career in merchandising.

Joffroy opened an office selling provisions to Southern Pacific, providing staples like San Francisco coffee, lard, tins of milk, sugar, beans and flour. He traveled around the country importing and exporting foodstuffs, at the mercy of crop failures, insects and governmental regulations. On one occasion an entire carload of garbanzo beans arrived in New York full of weevils, throwing Joffroy into a financial tailspin. He stayed in New York to recoup his investment and was able to negotiate a contract to sell 50 cars of dry foodstuffs.

By 1919 Alberto considered himself a playboy. He lived with his sisters on Torres Street and drove around town in a $4,000 baby blue Cadillac. He spotted Elinora Carreño at a dance at Nogales High School in 1919 and immediately knew, "This is the girl I'm going to marry."

Things weren't destined to be that easy.

Alberto and Elinora Joffroy's eight daughters

Elinora (Ellie) Joffroy Baffert
Mary Lou Joffroy Jones
Yolanda Joffroy Alfaro
Evangelina Joffroy Coppola
Estrella Joffroy Elias
Suzanna Joffroy Chernin
Roxanna Joffroy Barnett
Yvonne Joffroy Regan

The Joffroy family in 1946. Front row: Yolanda (on arm of sofa), Mary Lou, Alberto, Elinora, Ellie, Evangalina. Back row: Suzanna, Yvonne, Roxanna and Estrella.
Photo courtesy Suzanna Joffroy Chernin

Alberto and Elinora Joffroy in 1921.
Photo courtesy Suzanna Joffroy Chernin

Elinora Joffroy

Alberto Joffroy spotted Elinora Carreño at a dance at Nogales High School in 1919 and immediately knew his life would never be the same again. He arranged for a serenade, but when Elinora and her friends peeked out the window to see what he looked like, she said, "He's awful, look at all that five o'clock shadow." But she did agree to dance with him.

Alberto was so persistent that Elinora's father complained, "Wherever we go we keep running into this fellow, Joffroy." In the custom of the day, Alberto had to ask permission to visit her. He sent gifts, which her mother made her return, and finally sent for his brother in San Francisco to come to Nogales and ask for her hand. Señor Carreño's response was "No, she's too young and doesn't' know anything or even how to cook."

Elinora's parents had come to Mexico City from Seville, Spain and she was born there in 1901. Her father had a cigar factory in Mexico City and was a vice-president of the United Sugar Company. During the time of Pancho Villa, United Sugar moved its headquarters to El Paso causing the family to immigrate to the United States.

They moved to Nogales in 1914. Elinora was the oldest of ten children, eight born in Mexico and two in the U.S.

When Elinora was a baby, the family sailed from Vera Cruz to visit her grandmother in Spain. The little girl got seasick on the way home. A group of cloistered nuns on board took care of her during the passage. The nuns lived in a convent

Alberto and Elinora's wedding party gathered on the steps of her parents' home on West Street near Crawford, in Nogales, Arizona, Sept. 12, 1921.
Photo courtesy Suzanna Joffroy Chernin

school and taught the children in French. Elinora went to visit them at the age of three and went back later to attend school there until she was 13.

The Carreños' upbringing was very strict. Elinora's mother wouldn't let the girls go to any dances. When each became old enough, she took them to Los Angeles to register for boarding school. The boys were sent to a military academy. Elinora graduated from high school in 1920 and applied to Vassar, but her mother wouldn't let her go away.

Alberto and Elinora were married Sept. 12, 1921 at Sacred Heart Church in Nogales. Their first child, Ellie Joffroy Baffert, was born nine months and seven days later at their home on Walnut Street. She was the first of eight daughters; all delivered at home except for the youngest, who was born at the Stork's Nest in Tucson.

Alberto was ten years older than Elinora. He supported many relatives and had a lot of responsibilities. His older brothers didn't have much business sense, so he helped with their families and also took care of his sisters. He was nervous about bringing more children into the family but after the twins, Suzanna and Roxanna, were born, things got better. Alberto promised, "They will change our luck. We will go up from here."

And so they did. They were blessed with a rich and rewarding family life. The childrens' clothes were made at home by a seamstress, and the parents were able to travel to Mission Beach for a vacation every year and send all their children to college.

Through all Alberto's ups and downs with his various business dealings, local banker and financier Wirt Bowman, remained his steadfast friend. On many occasions, Bowman would float one of Joffroy's endeavors on the strength of his handshake alone, a testament to the strong bond of mutual trust between the two men.

In addition to his own business, Comestibles, S.A., Alberto helped relatives get established. He helped start Joffroy Customs House for his brother Alexander and helped his daughter and son-in-law Suzanna and Hugh Chernin establish Joffroy's Imports and Maya de Mexico in Nogales, Sonora.

On their 60th wedding anniversary in 1981, the Joffroy's youngest daughter Yvonne interviewed her parents for a video on their life together. She handed her father the mike and he said, "I'm the patriarch, but Mama's the boss." He added that the high point of his life was all the trips that he and his wife took after he retired, and all the family weddings and first communions. The low point was when they lost their daughter, Estrella, at the age of 38 from lupus.

The couple summed up their secret to a successful marriage with this thought, "We did it the old-fashioned way - it's better to give than to receive."

Elinora Joffroy died in 1985 and Alberto followed in 1986. In addition to their eight daughters, they left behind a legacy of 26 grandchildren and 18 great grandchildren. And a wonderful straw hat that is prominently displayed in the family room in the home of their daughter and son-in-law, Suzanna and Hugh Chernin.

Suzanna and Hugh Chernin treasure one of her father's trademark hats, displayed in the family room at their home east of Nogales.
Betty Barr photo

Maria Monteverde and Carlos Dávila on their wedding day. Ca 1929.
Photo courtesy Mercedes Dávila Jordan

Mercedes Davila Jordan

Mercedes Dávila was the daughter of Carlos Dávila Zayas, who served as the mayor of Guaymas in the early 1920s. He was a Diputado or a Representative of State, a position similar to a Congressman. Dávila moved to Los Angeles around 1917 when the rebels rose up against the Governor. He was unsuccessful in learning to speak English, but he had the good fortune to meet and marry Maria Monteverde.

The Monteverde family originally came from a section of northern Italy near the Swiss Alps. They lost their land and silver mines in Mexico, and during the revolution moved to Los Angeles. Maria was about 18 when she and Carlos married.

The young couple went to Nogales, Sonora to live and their five oldest children were born there. Maria did not work outside the home. In those days there were a lot of people to help with the big families and they always had a nanny to help with the children and the housework. When the Mexican government began a campaign of religious persecutions in the late 1920s the family returned to Los Angeles, where their daughter, Mercedes was born in 1930. There were eight children born to the family. Guadalupe (Lupita Dávila as she was known in Nogales), Ofelia, Maria Elena, Carlos, Luis, Roberto, Mercedes and Jose.

The Dávila name was originally Ávila in Spanish, and is familiar to Catholics because of the association with Teresa of Ávila. Grandfather Dávila was from Puebla. He met his wife, Mercedes' grandmother, in Alamos, a silver mining area and the first capital of Sonora. After their marriage the elder Dávilas settled in Guaymas. He was a pharmacist and politician and came on horseback to visit the family in Nogales.

The younger Dávila family moved back to Nogales, Sonora when Mercedes was about a year old. Her father was also a pharmacist but had lost his money during the Depression. He had discovered a medication similar to Alka Seltzer but didn't get a patent and never received any royalties from his invention, although the remedy is still sold in Mexico.

During Prohibition, Carlos Dávila's brothers started liquor stores in Sonora, where Carlos went to work in 1931 or 1932. He was content to be a clerk, and his brothers didn't give him a partnership in the business. The store was called Dávila Hermanos Liquor Shop. It was on Elias Street near where La Roca is now located.

Mercedes went to public school in Sonora for first and second grade. The government had closed all the Catholic churches and schools and confiscated all their treasures. When her mother heard that the four young, unmarried Macías sisters had come to Nogales, Arizona and started a school called Escuela Macías, she enrolled Mercedes there for third grade. Three of the sisters taught at the school. The fourth sister was blind and kept to herself most of the time. Their niece, Catalina, also taught there. Mercedes had her appendix out and missed a lot of class time. The teachers said she could come back in the summer and make up her tests, but her mother said, "No, she is too little," so she had to repeat the fourth grade.

Mercedes and her brother crossed through the border gate openly every day to go to school and return home. Her friends, sisters Laura and Maria Guadalupe López Chávez walked to school with them. Laura and Mercedes have been lifelong friends since the first day they met in 1940. Laura says, "Mercedes was the second little girl I met when my family moved from Guanajuato to Nogales and we have been like sisters ever since." None of them knew much English and Laura remembers that Mercedes' mother, who was born in Los Angeles and spoke fluent English, helped them tremendously. "She worked with us after school on our lessons and taught us the language so we could do well in school," Laura said.

The Escuela Macías was on Sonoita Street behind the Customs House and had a large patio in the center. All the students at the school were from Sonora, but during the summer, the American public school students took Spanish classes there. The living quarters for the Macías sisters were in the rear. The sisters were

Maria and Carlos Dávila with their children, back row: Lupita, Ofelia, Maria Elena, Carlos and Luis. Front row: Roberto, Mercedes and baby Jose. Ca. early 1930s.
Photo courtesy of Mercedes Dávila Jordan

very religious and often invited the priest to come and give instruction in the patio of the school. Mercedes made her first communion at St. Joseph convent next door when she was seven or eight.

When Mercedes was in fifth grade, Father Ignacio "Nacho" de la Torre, pastor of La Purisima Concepcion, was the only priest left in Sonora. The church had been closed during the religious revolution and Father Nacho started fund raising efforts to build a new church and school. Mercedes' sister Lupita was a musician and could do the traditional dance "La Borrachita," portraying a drunken old woman. To help raise funds for Father Nacho's new church, Lupita sang in the streets of Sonora while volunteers sold tamales. The new church was called El Santuario de Nuestra Señora de Guadalupe.

Mercedes' aunt, Eugenia Dávila, married Francisco Castillo Nájera, a general in the Revolutionary Army, who was also a medical doctor. He was the ambassador from Mexico to Washington, DC under Franklin Delano Roosevelt. According to Mercedes' friend Laura López (Murphy), "Eugenia was an elegant lady who carried her lap dog around in a hat box." Aunt Eugenia invited Mercedes' older sister, Lupita, to visit her in Washington, DC. Lupita, a social butterfly, met many people during her stay, including her future husband, Rogelio Alfaro, a Panamanian.

Alfaro had started the human rights movement in Panama. He graduated from Georgetown and served in France during the Second World War. He got an MBA and was the first one to open Central America and Panama for IBM. His father Don Ricardo Alfaro, was the ambassador from Panama, and had previously been president of that country. Don Ricardo was a respected jurist, practiced international law and served as one of the judges at The Hague.

Don Ricardo had helped to write the constitution of Panama and was a tenured professor of law at the University of Panama, but he never put on airs. When the Alfaro family came to Nogales to meet the Dávilas, Maria was extremely anxious about entertaining this exalted personage in her modest home, but Don Ricardo was very charming and played games like cat in the cradle with Mercedes. She always remembered him as a tender and sweet man, unlike his wife who was very reserved.

Mercedes' brother Luis lives in Tucson and all his family are musical. He thinks they inherited the gift from Verdi, the noted musician from northern Italy, the birthplace of his mother's people. Rodolfo Campodónico, a well-known composer in Sonora, is related by marriage to the Dávila family. He wrote the "Club Verde Waltz" a hymn of the revolutionary movement. The government expatriated him and he died in Douglas.

Mercedes moved to Guadalajara when she was 41. She is a gourmet cook and learned the Sonora style of cooking growing up in Nogales. She was working as a hostess in a restaurant when her future husband came in for dinner, carrying a copy of Don Quixote. They started dating and she introduced him to Catholicism. They soon married, but after three short years he was diagnosed with lung cancer. Since he was retired military, they came to Davis Monthan Air Force Base Hospital in Tucson for his treatment. During his illness, they stayed with Mercedes' old friend Laura López Murphy for the first few months. Mercedes' husband died after eight months of treatment.

Mercedes had taught dancing and singing for 30 years and after her husband passed away, she resumed that career. She taught Spanish dancing and flamenco in the bi-lingual program at Pima College. Once a week she traveled to Nogales and gave lessons, arranged by Susie Joffroy (Chernin), upstairs in the old Valley Bank building on Grand Avenue. She has since moved back to Guadalajara.

Border Patrol Agent Lon Parker, shown here in his WWI army uniform in 1917, was ambushed and killed by smugglers in Korn Canyon in the Huachuca Mountains in 1926.
Photo courtesy Byrd Lindsey

Lon Parker

In a remote area of the Huachuca Mountains near Bartel Springs, a huge boulder embedded with a plaque memorializes the murder of legendary Border Patrol Agent Lon Parker. The area is as rugged and inaccessible today as it was on that fateful Sunday, July 25, 1926 when young Parker set out without his partner to apprehend whiskey smugglers spotted in the region. It is so inaccessible in fact, that the marker was erected several miles west of Korn Canyon, the actual scene of the killing.

Steve Lindsey, whose father was Lon Parker's nephew, said, "He had taken one of the first jobs with the border patrol in Arizona, and as I understand it, the problems in those days weren't with drugs, but with liquor that the illegals would make and then smuggle over the Huachuca Mountains to sell on Fort Huachuca."

The fateful day had started out peacefully with Lon, his wife Georgia and stepmother Addie Musgrave Parker enjoying a picnic near their Canelo home with a group of friends. John Merritt, a neighbor well known as an experienced tracker, gave Parker a tip that some whiskey runners would be passing through Korn Canyon later that day. He offered to show Parker where he had spotted the tracks of a heavily-laden horse. He added that he noticed that the rider got off now and then to lead the animal up the steeper parts of the trail.

Parker thought the lead sounded promising and although protocol demanded that agents work in pairs, he feared that the smugglers would get away and decided not to wait for his partner, Albert Gatlin, to return from an assignment in the San Rafael Valley. Once Merrit pointed out the tracks, the pair parted ways, and Parker went on alone, accompanied only by his hound, Bugle. He would not be seen alive again.

Brothers Domitilio and Artilio Espinosa, along with their accomplice Negrecito, ran a mescal smuggling operation between Santa Cruz, Sonora and Fort Huachuca. The brothers lived part of the time in Lyle Canyon and on a previous occasion Parker had caught them and whipped them with his quirt. There was no love lost between the Espinosas and Lon Parker.

From evidence the Border Patrol pieced together at the scene, it appeared that the trio saw Parker following them and planned a trap. Domitilio and Negrecito positioned themselves in the thick oak and cypress stands along the trail, while Artilio continued slowly up the trail leading the pack. Suddenly a shot rang out. Parker was hit in the back with a bullet from a .30-30 rifle and knocked from his horse. The severely wounded agent pulled his revolver and shot Artilio through the forehead, then fired again and killed one of the packhorses. Domitilio and Negrecito fled the scene.

Parker mounted his horse and rode to Tom Will's place but the camp was empty. Lacking the strength to open the gate, he crawled through the barbed wire fence and made it as far as the woodpile before losing consciousness. When Wills returned home later in the afternoon, he found Parker's horse, the saddle stained with blood, and Parker lying unconscious, unable to tell what had happened.

The following morning Blain Lewis, a rancher from Sunnyside, led a team of investigators to the site of the killing. According to the Arizona Daily Star, July 27, 1926, "A party of officers consisting of Sheriff Harold Brown, Under-sheriff Pat Patterson and Deputy Jim Hathaway left Nogales at 11 p.m. for the scene of the shooting." They found Artilio Espinosa lying dead with a .30-30 rifle in his hands and empty shell casings scattered around. The dead horse and four five-gallon cans of mescal were nearby. Buster Pyeatt, Frank Federico and Alex Gonzales buried the body, leaving the packsaddle as a grim reminder to future smugglers.

Parker was born in 1892 on his father's ranch in Lyle Canyon near Canelo. His grandfather, William Alexander Parker, settled what is now known as Parker Canyon in the 1880s. Christened William Alonzo Parker, "Lon" grew up working cattle alongside his brothers Jim, John and Elmer. His mother, Eva Landers died when Lon was seven years old and his sisters, Pearl and Eunice, were sent

Group in front of the two-story adobe originally called the McDaniel House located far out in Brushy Canyon. From left, Jewel Maloney, Anna Parker, Jasper Joiner, three unidentified people. Far right, William "Uncle Billy" Parker. 1920s
Photo courtesy Byrd Lindsey

to live with relatives.

In 1905 Lon's father, affectionately referred to as "Uncle Billy Parker," married Adanna "Addie" Musgrave who later served as postmistress at Canelo. After enlisting as a gunnery sergeant in World War I, and a brief stint as a Santa Cruz County Deputy, Lon took the Border Patrol examination in Los Angeles and was accepted as a patrol inspector on September 26, 1924.

Parker's bravery and daring exploits began to make a name for him almost immediately. After only one month of service he and two other officers were scouting for illegal activity in the Huachuca Mountains when Parker discovered tracks of a pack train leading up Korn Canyon, just a short distance from the Mexican border.

The other officers had fanned out some distance away, and Parker followed the trail without backup. He suddenly found himself the target of gunfire.

Armed only with a revolver, Parker returned fire until he ran out of ammunition and then boldly charged the firing bandits, tackling and disarming Alvino Barboa. He wrestled Barboa's rifle away, shot him in the leg, then wounded one of the fleeing bandits in the thigh as the two of them ran off into the brush. When his fellow officers arrived on the scene, Parker said, "Sorry, but you're too late for the fun." He then looked down at the rifle Barboa had been carrying and realized it was the one that had been stolen from "Uncle Billy's" ranch earlier that same day.

The following year Parker was on patrol in the Baboquivari Mountains northwest of Nogales along with officers Herbert Wood, Philip Raymond, Quince Leatherman, William McKee and Deputy Sheriff Billy Gates. They intercepted three mounted men driving six packhorses loaded with cans of liquor. The bootleggers abandoned the pack train and fled, managing to elude capture.

After loading the liquor into their vehicles, the agents started to drive out of the mountains but had only traveled about two miles when the bootleggers attacked, killing McKee and wounding Wood. The bandits again raced off on horseback. Parker and Leatherman commandeered two of the pack mules and gave chase, but were unable to catch up with the outlaws. Returning to Nogales, Parker and Chief Patrol Inspector Walter Miller conducted an investigation that led to the capture of two of the bandits at the Perron Ranch near San Xavier Mission.

Parker provided key testimony and drawings of the murder scene at the preliminary hearing, leading Inspector Miller to say, "it (Parker's testimony) was of such a nature to make his life unsafe in the presence of any of the smugglers not intercepted by officers in the McKee case."

Two months later, in July of 1926, the pressure from the Border Patrol in the area pushed the contraband trail from the Baboquivaris back to the Hauchuca Mountains and Parker returned to his old stomping grounds where his fate awaited him.

For eight decades nothing but Artilio Espinosa's packsaddle and a crude cairn that had fallen into disrepair marked the spot where Parker suffered his fatal gunshot wound. In July 2006 about 100 people attended the dedication of the new memorial marking the 80th anniversary of the murder. Assistant Patrol Agent in Charge of the Naco Station, Chief Wayne Lackner, conducted the ceremony, which included the mounted B-Troop, in their Dragoon uniforms, and the Border

Three past and present Border Patrol agents coordinated the dedication of the site of Agent Lon Parker's murder on July 25, 1926. From left are Agents Wayne Lackner, Jim Grasky and Carl Norton. July, 2006.
Photo courtesy Border Patrol Agent Wayne Lackner

Patrol honor guard dressed in kilts and playing the bagpipes.

The site had first been dedicated in 1993 due to the efforts of since-retired Sonoita Agent Jim Grasky and Tucson Sector Horse Patrol Coordinator, Carl Norton, but the memorial had deteriorated with time. Grasky and Norton teamed up with Lackner to spearhead a more permanent testament to Parker's courage and dedication. They enlisted the help of Phelps Dodge Lavender Pit in Bisbee to provide the boulder and the Tucson Section, which funded the plaque. The marker is a permanent testament to Parker's bravery and serves as a reminder to modern-day agents to always work in pairs in the field.

Two months after Lon Parker's death, riders discovered Domitilio Espinosa's body about 300 yards from the ambush site. He had been shot between the eyes by an unknown avenger.

Lon Parker

By Steve Lindsey
December, 1997

Back in 1926
Before this State was tame,
There was a border patrolman,
Lon Parker was his name.

He worked the Huachuca Mountains,
The same place he called home,
Guess that's one of the reasons
They caught him there alone.

He got word one morning,
There was some wetbacks with a load,
And he didn't wait for back-up,
He just saddled up and rode.

He took his hound dog with him,
To help find the smugglers trail,
Cuz when it came to catching something,
That 'ole dog just couldn't fail.

He rode up past Tom Wills camp,
Got there about midday,
He figured at anytime now
He'd hear that hound dog bay.

He rode up through Korn Canyon,
And just below the peak,
That hound dog sure found something,
Just listen to him speak!

He rode across the water,
around a bend and sitting there
where he could see,
Was a horse and a whiskey smuggler,
Hunkered down underneath a tree.

"Buenos dias Senor Lon,"
the Mexican said real low,
Lon knew that there was something wrong,
But just what he didn't know.

"Donde esta su compadre?"
Lon asked when he heard the rifle crack,
And he felt the bullet's fury
Enter in his back.

Well, Lon he pulled his pistol
And shot the smuggler in the head,
Then he shot the smuggler's horse
And they both lay there dead.

Then he turned to find his killer,
But that coward had tucked his tail and run,
He didn't want to be seen when
Lon pulled the trigger on his gun!

Lon was getting weak now,
Blood was makin' his shirt damp,
So he figured he better try
To get back to Tom Wills' camp.

But no one was home there,
And on Tom's woodpile is where Lon died,
They found him there that evening,
The hound dog by his side.

Now this true story doesn't end there,
Someone killed the Mexican too,
But of all the people that I ask,
No one is real sure who.

They found him in Lyle Canyon,
He was laying there dead.
I guess we'll never know
Who shot him in the head.

Reprinted with permission from Steve Lindsey

Cowboy, Blain Lewis, at Parker Canyon in the early 1920s.
Photo courtesy Wanda De La Ossa.

Blain Lewis

They called him the last of the true old-time cowboys, but his real passion was horses according to his daughter Wanda De La Osa. "Dad loved his cows, but he really loved his horses. He bred them, broke them, rode them, showed them and raced them," she said. And he did it all with a flair and finesse that will not soon be forgotten in southeastern Arizona.

Blain's father, who was known simply as B, participated at Sonoita when locals founded the track and rodeo grounds in 1915. B ran the match races and brought the first good stud to the county in 1920. Blain rode in those first Sonoita races at the early age of nine. He started training racing horses when he won the first race ever run at the Santa Cruz County Fair & Rodeo Association track in Sonoita. He was only 17.

Blain trained for many others, but the best horses he trained were his own. One of his most famous studs, Parker's Trouble, helped boost Lewis' name to the top of the horse breeders' list. Parker's Trouble ranked No.3 in the country as a quarter horse sire. Parker's Trouble, with Blain, as trainer/breeder, was listed in the Quarter Horse Hall of Fame as Top Stud All Around Horse.

Parker's Trouble may have been the most famous of Blain's horses, but his favorite was his first stud, Texas B. Texas B could do everything - rope, race, show and run barrels, called bending in those days. Trouble Gal, Bit-O-Trouble, Bit-O-String and Bessy's String, who won a $4,000 futurity race in the early 1970s, were some of his other top-notch racehorses.

Blain Lewis rides the barrels on Texas B, his favorite stud horse, at the Sonoita Fairgrounds. In those days the event was called bending.
Photo courtesy Wanda Lewis De La Ossa.

Blain, who rode every day until he was 88, was featured in the Quarter Horse Journal as a Horseman of the Month. He raised Herefords and branded them with the H Spear, reserving the Double Staple brand for his horses

Bit-O-Trouble wins the 350 yard race at Rillito Race Track in Tucson on New Year's Eve, 1955. Blain Lewis, owner/trainer.
Courtesy Wanda Lewis De La Ossa.

Blain Lewis and Lonnie Hunt plow the fields at the Sunnyside homestead in 1930.
Photo courtesy Donnie Lewis Martin

Blain was born in 1905 in New Mexico. His family came to southeastern Arizona in a covered wagon in 1912. It was a 30-day trip on dirt cattle trails and 7-year old Blain rode a horse alongside the wagon to help keep things running smoothly. Their first night in Arizona was spent at the base of Parker Canyon, in what is now Parker Lake. His father started a ranch and Blain enrolled in the Parker Canyon School, which he attended through 8th grade. As a teenager he broke broncs for neighboring ranchers. In those days they waited until the horses were four years old, instead of two, so the animals were much harder to handle. He got $10 a head and was proud that he was seldom thrown off.

Lewis was elected to three terms as Santa Cruz County Supervisor and served for 39 years as State Livestock Inspector, but perhaps his best-known position was deputy sheriff and Patagonia town constable, positions he held for 10 years. Most of his calls were to handle drunks getting into fights. "It was all bars then. Most anything would get 'em angry and that would start 'em off," he told an Arizona Republic reporter in 1994. He was talking about the miners from Harshaw,

Blain Lewis shinning up the pole at Parker Canyon School in 1918. Photo courtesy Donnie Lewis Martin.

Mowry, Washington Camp, and Duquesne, which are all ghost towns today.

Then came April 29, 1945. Blain ran into the Mexican wife of Herman, "Old Man," Bender, in Patagonia and asked about his friend, who hadn't been seen in several days. The 70-year-old Bender was supposedly the richest man in Duquesne and when his young wife claimed that he had gone to Old Mexico for his heart, "I knew that wasn't so," Lewis told a Tucson reporter.

He immediately enlisted three men for a posse. Accompanied by his brother, Greet Lewis, Lloyd Gatlin and Henry Acevedo, Lewis went out to Bender's place

Deputy Sheriff Blain Lewis. Lewis served for ten years as deputy and constable in Patagonia in the 1930s and '40s.
Photo courtesy Donnie Lewis Martin

and started looking for clues. Blain began tracking in the area and found blood on the timbers at the entrance to a mineshaft on Bender's property. He went a short way into the shaft and smelled Prince Albert pipe tobacco inside, Bender's favorite brand. He also saw some gray hairs caught on the sides of the shaft.

Since the posse didn't have the equipment to retrieve what they were sure was Bender's body at the bottom of the shaft, they went for help. Justice of the Peace, Oliver Rothrock, and three miners from the Trench Mine arrived with equipment to aid in the recovery effort. They found the body lying in a pool of cold water at 250'. He had been shot in the head and the body was mutilated.

They were only able to ID Bender from his clothes and the can of his favorite

Sheriff Blain Lewis (second from right) keeps the peace at the Big Steer Saloon in Patagonia. Right is Lewis' son Iree, on his other side is Little Bob Haverty. Ca 1940s.
Photo courtesy Donnie Lewis Martin

Prince Albert, caught in rocks down the side of the pit. His much younger wife, Librada, who was only 32, denied any knowledge of how her husband had ended up in the bottom of the shaft. Librada had a reputation as a heavy drinker and the jury was unconvinced of her innocence. It was believed that she enlisted the aid of her two nephews to murder her husband to get more money to continue on a drinking spree.

Librada was sentenced to life and died in prison several years later. Her nephews, Richard Rodriquez and Benito Arias received 20 years. Many years later, one of the boys came back to Patagonia after his release. Donnie Martin, Blain's daughter, remembers being scared, fearing that he would try to get revenge on her father.

In his later years, Lewis' daughter-in-law, Jean, took him to the Stage Stop Inn every Tuesday for lunch. People knew of his routine and would stop by to visit with him and listen to his memories of the frontier days when he grew up in the area. What he missed most about the old days, were the neighborliness and friendship that was the hallmark of the area. Families would get together every weekend for country dances and picnics where everyone was invited. And he missed his active lifestyle. "I sure wish I could still ride my horse," he said at one lunch gathering. Most of all Lewis missed his wife Laura, who passed away in 1992.

May Gates spearheaded the 80th birthday party for Blain Lewis, held at the Sonoita Fairgrounds in 1985 and presented him with a money tree of $692. The tree was rooted in a wheelbarrow full of manure. Gates told him he could keep the money, but she wanted the manure for her garden. Hettie Lee Gardner, center, congratulates Blain and his wife Laura.
Photo courtesy of Donnie Lewis Martin.

THE HORSE BREEDER

By Paul Duffey

There lives a man near Patagonia town
Whose horse breeding has won him renown.
He came to these parts when just a boy
And grew up to be a real cowboy.

He's a lean man with saddle-bowed legs,
Who raises and shares farm-fresh eggs.
His favorite stud, Charger is named.
Many's the colt he's bred and tamed.

His first horse was Punkin
Which he gave to his kin.
Texas B was an all-around winner-
His racing won Blain many a dinner.

Parker's Trouble was a race horse
Until he got lame. Blain broke him
For riding, and put him out to stud.
He took to that role with vigor and vim.

He sired many winners of quarter horse fame
Big Step, Bit 0Trouble, Trouble Gal by name.
Pima Country and others, many as he could.
His speed, action, disposition all good.

Blain has survived well over many a year
But not without an occasional tear.
Floods and snows, droughts and rains
Banks and tough guys have given him pains.

Those who know him find him to be
Kind and gentle, to you and to me.
So let's all give a big Hooray"
For Blain Lewis's 80th birthday!

8/9/85

Sweethearts Blain Lewis and Laura Dunham. He was 21 and she was 19 when they married in 1926.
Photo courtesy Wanda De La Ossa.

Laura Dunham Lewis

Laura Dunham was born in Alabama. Her family moved to Mowry when she was a small child, where her father, T. G. Dunham, hauled ore for the mine. In 1913, T. G. and his wife, Ellen, applied for a homestead in the San Rafael Valley. Laura went to the San Rafael one-room school and then moved to Nogales where she lived with Rev. and Mrs. O. A. Smith so she could attend Nogales High School. She cooked and cleaned for them to earn her room and board.

She married Blain Lewis, who was working for Circle Z Guest Ranch, in 1926. She was only 19. They soon bought a place in Sunnyside from John Jones and started their own ranch. Laura learned to drive so she could get the mail route from Sunnyside to Patagonia.

The Great Depression hit and they lost the Sunnyside ranch in 1933. This was the beginning of a series of hardships and disappointments. Blain drove his remaining 400 head of cattle to Tucson to graze on the desert grasses, but most of them died from eating poisonous burro weed. The young family moved on to San Simon and filed for a homestead, but couldn't find water. Fortunately, Blain was able to land a job with Santa Cruz County working on the roads, and the couple returned to the Patagonia area.

Lewis worked for Henry Boice as a foreman at the Rail X Ranch until it was sold, and then bought the 600-acre Red Rock property. His first well was bad so he drilled another, and eventually put in five wells on the property, ranging from 50 – 500' deep. The Lewis family, including all Blain and Laura's children, their

T. G. and Ellen Dunham, with two of their nine children, Laura and Ray, resting under the big oak behind their homestead in the San Rafael Valley. Ca. 1913 – 1920. Photo courtesy Donnie Lewis Martin.

T. G. Dunham's road camp at the Mowry mine sometime between 1910 and 1920. Dunham hauled ore for the mine and homesteaded in the San Rafael Valley. He was the father of Laura Lewis.
Photo courtesy Donnie Lewis Martin.

spouses and grandchildren have lived continuously at the ranch since 1935.

Laura applied for her old mail route in the San Rafael Valley and delivered the mail six days a week over curving mountainous roads, a 96 mile round trip. She always took her pre-school children with her and there never was a day that the mail didn't get through in her 42 years of driving. She made about 75 stops, some on roads that were no more than cart tracks, so her cars would only last for two or three years. She sometimes waited for hours for a creek to subside and at least one time didn't get back to Patagonia until 9 p.m., after a twelve-hour day.

Laura and Blain Lewis with one of the many cars that she wore out driving the San Rafael Valley mail route. In 2008, the route had remained in the Lewis family for 74 years.
Photo courtesy Donnie Lewis Martin.

"There was always someone to help you if you needed it," Laura told reporter Alma Ready in 1972. "The houses are scattered out, but you can see a long distance. From the San Rafael headquarters you can see for miles in four directions, and the foreman knew that if he saw my dust in one place an I didn't show up in another, I must be stuck somewhere in between. Then he would send somebody out to help me."

The mail route has remained in the family ever since, for a total of 74 years. Daughter, Wanda De La Osa, had the route for 14 years, with her sister Donnie Martin and neighbor Dusty Hudson, substituting for her at times. Wanda turned it over to her nephew Jim Lewis' wife, Dawn, who by 2008 has delivered for 18 years.

Blain passed away in 1995 at age 90. Laura had died several years previously. The couple had four children, Jesse, Donnie, Iree and Wanda, and many grandchildren and great-grandchildren. Blain played the fiddle at local gatherings and the whole family loves to dance. "He was a very wild young cowboy (who) my mother had to tame. She said that when he was young he could dance a jig that was unreal," Wanda said.

Laura Lewis hangs the wash on a makeshift clothesline at the family ranch in Red Rock Canyon in the late 1940s.
Photo courtesy Donnie Lewis Martin.

Slim Mayo with his horse Fox in the early 1940s.
Photo courtesy of Kathy Nell Mayo.

Slim Mayo

A tall, skinny cowboy leaning against his family's disabled vehicle near Cortaro Farms Road caught the eye of a woman driving by. Pulling over she hollered, "If you know anything about horses, I'll pay you $25 a month to work at the Glover Ranch in Avra Valley." "Ma'am, I know all about horses," the 24-year-old James "Jim" Mayo drawled.

He was hired on the spot. The Glovers already had a Jim working for them, so they dubbed him "Slim." Measuring 6'2" tall and weighing in at 160 pounds dripping wet, he could not have been given a better name.

Slim Mayo and his parents had pulled up stakes in Oklahoma and were heading for California to look for work when they found themselves stranded in Tucson on that fateful day in 1936. Slim had recently been discharged from the army where he had served in the 18th Field Horse Drawn Artillery at Ft. Sill, Oklahoma. After he landed the job at Glover Ranch his father found work at the University of Arizona Farms and the family decided to make Arizona their home.

Slim was born in Mississippi in 1912 and grew up in rural Oklahoma. He was riding his own horse, carrying his own rifle and working at his first paying job, driving a team that pulled a hay baler, by the age of six. He earned $1 a day. Within two years, he was pulling a hayrack on a neighbor's spread with a team of mules. To look more "grown up," he and the other boys would buy bags of Bull Durham tobacco and let the tags hang out of their pockets. The family grew their own vegetables, raised chickens, milk cows, beef and pork. They charged their staples at the market and paid off the bill when they sold hogs or cattle.

Shortly after arriving in Arizona, Slim came to the attention of the film director, Wesley Ruggles, who was shooting a motion picture on location at Old Tucson. Ruggles asked Slim to manage the livestock, drive the wagon teams and do stunt work for the movie, "Arizona," starring William Holden and Jean Arthur. They brought the bull wagons up from Mexico and pawned them off as oxen in the movie. The crew used the cattle so hard that their hooves got sore. Slim told how he had to shoe the longhorn bulls so the shooting could stay on schedule. When they ran out of shoes they cut horseshoes in half and formed them up to fit the bulls.

The following year, Slim met Kit and Buel Hutchinson, recent transplants from Chicago who had bought a ranch in the San Rafael Valley. The couple planned

Slim Mayo with his mother at the Tucson Railroad Station. When Slim discovered that one of the local bars didn't let rowdy cowboys in the door, he bought himself a fancy fedora to look more sedate. Ca late1930s.
Photo courtesy Kathy Nell Mayo.

to start a boarding school and needed help getting all the necessary permits and a wrangler to tend livestock. Slim was a natural for the job. Kit said, "Slim had been working somewhere and smelled like it!" She told him, "We'll have you smelling like a rose in no time."

From day one, Slim and the Little Outfit were a perfect combination. For the first through eighth graders, many of them asthmatic boys who had been sent to Arizona for the healthy, clean air, Slim was a bigger-than-life cowboy, a combination of John Wayne and Gary Cooper. He played the guitar and the harmonica at the same time, could ride anything with four legs and told tall tales that rivaled anything the kids had seen on the silver screen.

The school included a dormitory, the main ranch house, one-room school, dairy, 20 horses and a barn. The young wrangler was soon enlisted to teach the students to ride and rope, shoe horses and repair tack. Slim showed them how to throw

In 1917 Harry Fryer homesteaded the property that later became the Little Outfit Ranch School. He lived nearby and often worked with the students. Here he teaches students how to pan for gold and shows them a gold nugget that turned up in his pan. Ca 1945.
Photo courtesy Don Dean.

a diamond hitch over the loads on the animals in the pack string, track wildlife and roll a cigarette single-handed. Don Dean, a former student remembers, "Slim had his own little cabin down the hill and he was always available if one of us needed an adult to talk to. He would strum his guitar and listen to our troubles. He taught us self-confidence, perseverance and how to be a man."

During spring and fall roundups, the boys were allowed to help at neighboring ranches. Slim said, "They made pretty good cowboys, those little boogers." According to Dean, "Under Slim's guidance a lot of us became very good horsemen and expert marksmen. We each had a horse and saddle of our own. After lunch, Slim put us through half an hour of military drill and then we rode horses the rest of the day. We took weekly pack-trips to Parker Canyon or Lochiel or went on campouts in the Huachucas." Harry Fryer, who homesteaded the Little Outfit property in 1917, lived nearby and often joined Slim to help out on these excursions

Slim stayed at Little Outfit about 10 years, with time out to train pack mules for the army in 1942. He was packing supplies to ski troops on bivouac in the Rocky Mountains when a mule slipped on the ice and fell on him, breaking his foot. He received a medical discharge and returned to the Little Outfit in 1943. His salary was $150 a month, compared to other cowboys in the area who usually earned $50 to $70.

Slim met Katherine "Kay" Hollans several times at dances at the Elgin Club. Kay later attended productions at the Little Outfit with her aunt, Mrs. Sophie Boosinger, principal of Patagonia Elementary School. Slim had left the Little Outfit at the end of the school year, and was working at Frank Moson's Y Lightning, a well known cattle and guest ranch near Hereford, when the couple was married in 1947.

Slim told his daughter Kathy lots of stories about his time at the Y Lightning, including the reason he left. He said that one of his "jobs" had been to take the good-looking women guests on picnics, or to Fletchers Roundup for dances or down to Nick's in Hereford to gamble. Moson told him the women were either going to wear him down or tie him up and Slim figured this might be a good time to move on.

Moson had the best horses in the area. Two of them looked like twins, except that one was slightly larger than the other. One day another wrangler got the two mixed up. He saddled Happy, a very spirited animal, and put a dude on him by mistake. When the lady guest was promptly bucked off, Moson decided to get

Slim and Kay Mayo standing in front of their house in Canelo with their best man and maid-of-honor on their wedding day, Nov. 28, 1947. From left Jack Gowell, Slim and Kay Mayo, Johnie Gowell.
Photo courtesy Kathy Nell Mayo

rid of the animal.

Slim liked riding Happy and offered to trade a buckskin and another horse for him. The deal was made, but the buckskin whipped Moson's prize stallion in a race, humiliating Moson and his favorite stud. Moson was furious and lost no time in returning the animal. Slim ended up with both Happy, who became his favorite roping animal, and the buckskin.

He said that Happy was invaluable when he got the contract to handle the buffalo herd at Ft. Huachuca. The animals liked to gather around the water hole near the north gate, close to the impact range. Slim was charged with keeping the herd of 600 buffalo away from the area while the troops practiced firing mortars and artillery. He would drive them to the edge of Pyeatt's Ranch at the west end of the fort early in the day and let them return to water in late afternoon. "I could

Jack Gowell and Slim Mayo at the Canelo Store in 1947. The store also served as the post office and was a gathering place for the locals. Photo courtesy Kathy Nell Mayo.

run right over the buffalo with that horse," he told the Sierra Vista Herald in 1985, "I roped and doctored hundreds of them with Happy."

Over the years Slim worked at many ranches in the area, including the Little Boquillos near Fairbank, Mattie Johnson's ranch in Elgin and Sid Vale's ranch in the Chiricahuas, where he worked with the famous quarterhorse, Three Bars. From 1954 to 1974 he served as a firefighter with the Ft. Huachuca Fire Department. The firefighters worked one day on and one day off. For 17 years he used his days off to work at the Sands Ranch in Whetstone for foreman, Lou Ramsey.

When Red Sanders, another cowboy from the Sands Ranch, got married, Slim and Lou decided to help him celebrate. They passed around their bottle of liquor, but after the first round the cork got stuck in the neck. They all worked on it with their penknives, but no amount of prying would push it free. They set the bottle up on a table across the room and Red whipped out his pistol and shot the neck off. For the rest of the night, they strained the whiskey through a bandanna.

Slim's duties at the Sands Ranch were to check on the windmills and water holes and make sure the salt licks were put out. He had his own cabin in French Joe Canyon where he kept five horses and during the roundups he helped with the brandings. He, Red and Lou remained lifelong friends.

Slim Mayo and other legendary cowboys of the area are featured in an exhibit at the Henry Hauser Museum in the Ethel Berger Center in Sierra Vista. Slim's collection of saddles, camp gear, cooking utensils, tack, a calf-feeding bottle and photographs are on loan to the museum from his daughter, Kathy Mayo.

In 1992 seven former students of the Little Outfit got together for a "Little Outfitters" reunion and discovered that their hero, Slim Mayo, was still living in the area. The word spread and six years later 22 people traveled from across the world and the country to honor him one last time. Although very ill, he made good his vow to live long enough to see them again and share their memories of the old west of 50 years past. Slim passed away one week later on May 16, 1998.

Kathy Mayo at one year of age at the Mattie Johnson place where her father worked as foreman. Jim Hathaway gave her the burro because it was born one month to the day that Kathy was born. Hathaway was a self-made vet, or healer, and had saved the life of Mayo's dog, Jackalope by amputating his leg. The dog in this photo is the son of Jackalope.
Photo courtesy Kathy Nell Mayo

"Epitome"

By Kathy Nell Mayo

At a Canelo ranch named the Little Outfit
He inspired a bunch of kids
For they had seen their first real cowboy
And wanted to do the things he did.

He taught them about ropin', ridin' and riflery
And gave to each of them some soul
The kind that comes from inside a cowboy
That only their kind knows.

He taught them more than fundamentals
He taught them honesty, ethics and respect
For God's creatures and the great outdoors
That cowboys proudly call the Code of the West.

He became their legend
He was their John Wayne
He was their cowboy hero
Even though he had no famous name.

I call this poem "Epitome"
I think it's a fitting word
For of all the cowboys
He heads up the herd.

Excerpt reprinted with permission from Kathy Nell Mayo.

Kit "Pete" Hutchinson, owner of Little Outfit Ranch School in the San Rafael Valley. Ca. 1945.
Photo courtesy Don Dean

Kit and Buel Hutchinson
The Little Outfit Ranch School

"You have the big outfit and I have the little outfit. I think that's what I'll call it," Kit Hutchison told her friend, Dorothea Meigs. Kit and Buel Hutchinson, educators from Chicago, arrived in southeastern Arizona in 1940 looking for a location for a private boarding school for grades 1 – 8. They took a drive out to the remote San Rafael Valley to visit Meigs, an old friend who owned the J2 Ranch. They were enchanted by the views from a hillside overlooking miles of untouched rolling hills and grasslands that stretched to Mexico. They had found the perfect spot.

Meigs told them that a nearby ranch, homesteaded by Harry Fryer in 1917, was going to be available for sale. The couple purchased the land before it could be listed on the market. The schoolhouse, dormitory, and a ranch house with a dining hall were quickly finished, and the Little Outfit Ranch School opened Oct. 1, 1940.

Students arrived by train from cities all over the country. They were picked up at either the Tucson Railway Station or at what is now the ghost town of Fairbank. An approaching cloud of dust would signal the approach of either Kit or Buel, driving an International truck. The pickup was outfitted with slats on the sides that could hold up a tarp in inclement weather. Inside, two benches facing each other provided less than comfortable seating arrangements.

Before embarking on the 70-mile bumpy ride over dirt roads to the school, the Hutchinsons made an obligatory stop at Porter's Western Wear in Tucson. Every student was issued a cowboy hat, preferably black, a pair of boots, 5 pairs of Levis, a Levi jacket and a rope. Now properly outfitted, their transformation from city slickers to Little Outfitters had begun.

Teachers in jeans, Noell Todd (Toddy) and Irene Raffensberger (Raffs) ring the bell for the opening of school. 1944.
Photo courtesy Don Dean

Next stop was the Wagon Wheel Bar in Patagonia, 17 miles shy of their final destination. The boys were directed to seats at the counter. One of the barstools was wired with a Model-A coil, which sent an electric charge to the unfortunate "dude" who hitched himself up on the seat. At just that exact moment, Sheriff Blain Lewis, in a big ten-gallon hat, would swagger into the bar packing two .45s on his hip. This embarrassing indoctrination provided great amusement to the locals, but, for many impressionable boys, it marked the beginning of a life-altering experience that would shape their future as nothing before or since.

The Hutchinsons had two daughters who attended school at the Little Outfit the first few years, along with several girls from nearby ranches. Meigs' daughter, Barbara, rode her horse to classes every day. Two years later, it became an all-boys' school, and in 1944 a summer camp was added. The school was phased out in 1949, but the summer camp continued until 1952.

Katherine "Kit" Hutchinson was "The Boss." She dreamed the big dreams and made her vision of a boarding school for boys, many of them asthmatic and behind in school, a living, breathing reality. She could ride, rope and light a cigarette with one hand, but her tough exterior masked a warm heart. She often served as a mother figure for boys far away from home. The kids called her "Pete," a nickname given her by head wrangler, Slim Mayo, who said the way she rode reminded him of a soldier named Pete that he served with in the army.

Pete was an extraordinary English teacher, and quickly had the boys caught up to grade level in the subject, but her real passion was theatrical productions. She wrote songs and plays, taught the boys to sing, dance and act, and directed the productions. Her personality was so persuasive that the boys agreed to play the parts of girls when necessary to keep the action moving.

The stage consisted of a cement slab projecting from the rear of the schoolhouse, with the surrounding hills forming a natural amphitheater. Toward the end of the first school year, Kit invited all the neighboring ranch families and people from the surrounding towns to the first annual "Outfitters Outing." Almost 200 people arrived for an entire day of activities, including exhibitions of riding, marching, tumbling and track. Following a bar-b-q picnic, the day concluded with a dramatic production starring the students.

Alvessa Hummel and Fern Collie often provided the music for what became an annual event. In the early 1940s, the movie "Oklahoma" was filmed within a few miles of the Little Outfit, inspiring Kit to modify the words slightly for her own show. "Arizona" was performed to rave reviews.

Slim Mayo teaches the students how to play the guitar at the Little Outfit School. 1944
Photo courtesy Don Dean

Buel Hutchinson taught science, ran the business side of the school and liked to pretend that he was in charge. Although Pete ignored most of his advice, he was, in fact, the steadying influence behind the scenes. His father, Duke "Doc" Hutchinson, a retired Chicago doctor, served as the resident physician. The students claim they had an excellent incentive to stay healthy. They didn't trust his eyesight and were wary of his shaky hands.

The one-room school was open six days a week, October thru May, with a two-week break in February for the Tucson Rodeo and one day off for Christmas. There was no central heating in the schoolhouse so one of the teachers had to go over early and light a match to get the portable heater going. There were

Buel Hutchinson, owner of the Little Outfit Ranch School, takes a group of students to collect firewood near the creekbed leading to the spring behind the ranch. The wagon is pulled by two donkeys, Jack and Jenny. Ca. 1945.
Photo courtesy Don Dean

no phones, electricity was powered by a generator, and the boys traveled most places by horseback.

The staff included three teachers for math, English and social studies. One of the former students, Don Dean, said they were not allowed to read novels and the only reading material they had, outside of textbooks, was Life Magazine and National Geographic.

Their routine included a lot of horseback riding. Three afternoons a week, the boys went on two-hour rides and on weekends they camped out overnight in

Eighth-grader, Donnie Dean shows off his roping skills to his classmates in the corral at the Little Outfit Ranch School. Ca. 1944.
Photo courtesy Don Dean

Parker Canyon or Lochiel. In the spring and fall the boys helped the neighbors, including the Choates, McPhersons and Meigs, with cattle roundups. These were usually two or three-day events and the kids ate and slept outside.

Head wrangler, Slim Mayo, was the boys' hero. Slim was the ultimate cowboy. After class he taught them how to ride, rope a horse and brand cattle. Each boy had his own horse to care for and performed the chores usually handled by cowboys. Slim also taught military maneuvers and weapons handling. He was trained to give the boys emergency care, including injections, since he often took them camping to distant areas. He packed the medical supplies, along with a gun for rattlers, in his saddlebags.

Slim had his own living quarters, a small cabin on the property and was always available to the boys if they needed someone to talk to. He would strum his guitar and listen to their troubles. According to Dean, "He was a good musician, but not much of a singer. He sure wasn't Elvis Presley."

Each week, Slim graded the students on brains, brawn and bridle and posted their points on a chart. The hard-fought, yearlong battle culminated with the naming of the Top Hand, the student with the highest cumulative point score. The coveted award was considered the ultimate accomplishment for a Little Outfitter.

Dean remembered Slim teaching him to break two horses when he was only 11 years old. He started out on the ground leading them with the bridle and after five weeks Slim said he was ready. He got on Foxy, but the gelding put the brakes on and refused to move even when Dean kicked as hard as he could. To speed up the action, Slim whacked Foxy on the rump with his hat and he started bucking like crazy. Kit got worried and cussed Slim out but Dean stayed on. Afterwards Slim told him he wasn't worried, he knew Don could ride him down.

Dean's grandmother had sent him to the school, but she wanted him to work for the $750 per semester tuition. For .50 cents an hour he got up at 4:30 a.m. to feed the animals, milk the cows, separate the cream, feed the chickens, collect the eggs and muck out the stalls. He got all the chores done before joining the other students for breakfast. Every Saturday, Pete would give him .25 cents, which was enough to buy him a haircut and an ice cream cone in Patagonia.

In 2008, Dean contacted Peter Robbins, current owner of the Little Outfit Ranch, and proposed petitioning the Federal Government to list the old one-room schoolhouse on the National Register of Historic Sites. Robbins liked the idea and the Historic Site Committee was formed. Bill Leggett, along with Peggy Booth, widow of one of his classmates, headed up the effort, with help from Dean, John Guilbert and Dick Albert. According to Leggett, one-room schoolhouses for rural and ranch families were quite common but the Little Outfit was unique in that it was private and attracted new people to the area. The committee feels confident that their petition will be successful and the school's place in Santa Cruz County's history will be preserved.

Slim Mayo posts a student's score on the Top Hand bulletin board at the Little Outfit. Points were awarded for brains, brawn and bridle. 1944.
Photo courtesy of Don Dean

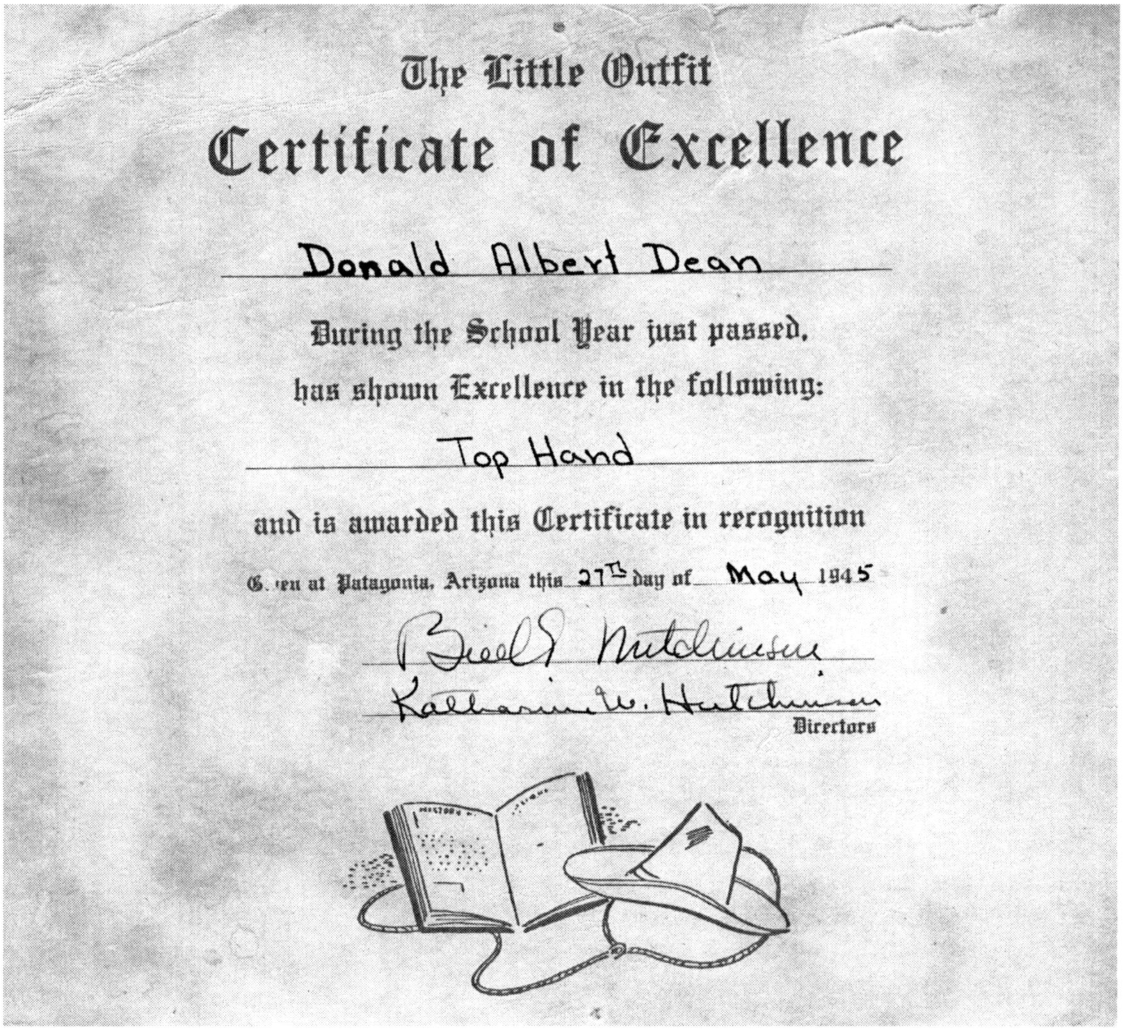

The Little Outfit

Certificate of Excellence

Donald Albert Dean

During the School Year just passed,
has shown Excellence in the following:

Top Hand

and is awarded this Certificate in recognition

Given at Patagonia, Arizona this 27th day of May 1945

Directors

Don Dean won the Top Hand certificate, the ultimate honor for a Little Outfitter, May 27, 1945. Courtesy Don Dean

Little Outfit students rode horseback from the ranch in the San Rafael Valley to the army base at Ft. Huachuca. The Apache Indians told them about their jobs as army scouts in front of the original cannon on the parade field. Ca mid-1940s.
Photo courtesy of Don Dean

Harold Thurber, president of the Arizona Hereford Association, and his registered Hereford bull check in at the front desk of the Santa Rita Hotel. The occasion was a national convention of the American Hereford Association held in Tucson in the late 1950s. Admiral Bull Halsey served as guest speaker.
Photo courtesy Bowman Archives Center

H. B. "Harold" Thurber

Harold Thurber should have been called "The Shipshape Man." He had served in the Navy, was a stickler for neatness and order and could be hard to please. It was said that he always had three crews, "One working, one coming and one going," according to Bill Piper. Despite this reputation, Piper, who had just graduated from Texas Tech, jumped at the chance for an interview when a feed company salesman he met at the Ft. Worth Stock Show told him that Thurber, owner of a large Hereford ranch north of Sonoita, was looking for a new ranch manager.

Piper came to Sonoita for an interview in May of 1952 and was offered the position. He said Thurber wanted to see every cow every day, and demanded a lot from his employees; however, it was no more than he was willing to do himself. "Harold was up almost every morning before daybreak to mix the feed, and after working a full day he would get cleaned up and head for Tucson for several hours of meetings. He wouldn't get back to the ranch until after dark, but he was up bright and early the next day without fail," his neighbor and fellow rancher, Bob Bowman, said.

Abel Molina was one of Thurber's best hands. He rode his horse over from Greaterville every day and staked him out in the field before starting to work. He built miles of the fence on the ranch and was insulted when he discovered that Thurber expected him to do yard and pool maintenance along with his other duties. When the Thurbers were expecting company, Molina had to clean the pool and mop the deck.

Harold Thurber looks on as his ranch manager, Bill Piper, tries on a new pair of Justin Boots at the ranch. The photo was used as an ad for Justin Boots that ran in the program at the Ft. Worth Livestock Show. Ca 1950s.
Photo courtesy Bill and Posy Piper

Harold Thurber was known as "Mr. Hereford." He was one of several people who showed cattle from this part of the state and he did a lot to make the breed well known and popular. "He wanted everything clean," Piper remembers There were four or five barns to keep clean and the hands were kept busy combing, brushing, trimming feet and giving shots. There were also nurse cows to take care of. In later years he imported purebred Herefords from England.

A production sale was held every year in the big show barn on the ranch. The barn was roomy enough to accommodate bleachers for buyers and spectators.

Thurber served food and beverages after the sale and everyone stayed to enjoy the relaxed atmosphere and talk over cattle prices and the weather.

The cover of the Herd Bull Edition of the American Hereford Journal featured a calf-branding picture that was taken on the ranch. The article mentioned Harold Thurber but neglected to give the name of his partner, Foy Herschede. This oversight caused bitter acrimony and Herschede withdrew from the partnership. Thurber's son Harold, Jr. went to work for Herschede at his ranching operation south of Sierra Vista near Palominas, but eventually returned to his father's ranch in Sonoita.

(From left) Bill Piper, Harold Thurber, Foy Herschede and Roland Poe show off the prize Hereford bulls. Ca 1952 –53.
Photo courtesy Bill and Posy Piper

Postcard showing aerial view of the Thurber and Herschede Ranch with a large inset of Hereford bull. Caption reads: M. W. Larry Domino, 116th & Thurber and Herschede Welcomes you to the Ranch at Anytime. Sonoita, Arizona. Ca 1950s.
Photo courtesy Bill and Posy Piper

Harold Thurber originally came to Arizona to recuperate from a lung problem that he likely contracted while serving in the U.S. Navy. He had been the skipper of a private yacht out of New York, which was pressed into service in the First World War, and he enlisted in the Navy at that time. He had recuperated at several different sanitariums before coming to Tucson for treatment at the Veteran's Hospital.

Upon arriving in Arizona, he bought his first ranch, now called the T-4, northeast of Nogales. He sold it shortly afterwards, moved briefly to Nevada, and then returned to Arizona, where he purchased a ranch from Roy Adams that he called Thurber Hereford Ranch. He later purchased property from Virgil Johnson which included the Buck Ranch, a house and small acreage north of his headquarters, and later acquired the Singing Valley property owned at one time by Gene Burns.

According to Bowman, Thurber painted all the wood surfaces at the ranch battleship gray. He had a landing strip on the property and painted his name in two to three-foot letters on the metal roof of the barn so that Hudgin Air Service could locate it when they picked him up to fly to meetings in Phoenix. On one occasion the pilot didn't get the wheels up in time and they caught on the barbed wire fence on take-off causing a minor wreck with no injuries.

Thurber shipped cattle by train to the Holcomb Hereford Farm in New York, escorted by his son Seymour. (From left) Bill Piper, H.B. Thurber, Dorothy Fisher, Seymour Thurber with his wife, child and a playmate. Ca 1950s.
Photo courtesy Bill and Posy Piper

Thurber and his neighbors the Bowmans provided housing for Up With People cultural exchange students touring the country. Four visiting girls enjoyed an Easter dinner at the Bowman home. (From left) Harold Thurber, Mary Bowman, four Up with People students, Bob Bowman. Ca. 1980s.
Photo courtesy Bob and Mary Bowman

Mary Bowman often tells the story of when she and Bob first moved to Sonoita. "We were living in the barn while we remodeled the house at our ranch. The barn was pretty rustic and the roof was flapping in the wind when Harold Thurber drove up. He introduced himself and said, 'I have an extra house on my property. Come stay there."

That was the beginning of a lasting friendship between neighbors. Every year the Thurbers hosted a party to celebrate February birthdays. Thurber and Mary Bowman shared a birthday on the 28th, and his foreman Bill Piper was born on February 27. "It was always a good party time," Posy Piper said. She added, "He had a kind heart and helped us out when our daughter was born with a blood problem. He was very generous to us."

Thurber was a natural born leader and seemed to always end up as organizer or president of every organization he joined. As chairman of the State Fair Board he was responsible for engaging performers for the Pima County Fair. When acts, such as the Osmond Family and others, applied to perform, Thurber asked them to audition in Patagonia. He used these "warm up" sessions to raise funds for the new hall for the Community Church in Patagonia. The grateful church members dedicated the new building Thurber Hall in recognition of his efforts.

He also served as President of Southern Arizona International Livestock Association (SAILA) and was instrumental in getting the Tucson Fairgrounds moved from South Sixth Avenue to its present location on Houghton Road.

Around 1934 Thurber became active in the Santa Cruz County Fair Association and used his fund-raising skills to get donations from his associates in Tucson. He was in charge of publicity and was also named to assist Charles Putnam, chairman of the poultry department. Poultry was one of his special interests, and he and his sons raised exotic birds at the ranch.

In 1936 Thurber was elected to the board of the Fair Association and helped spearhead the order revoking the original certificate of incorporation that had been issued May 8, 1915. The board re-incorporated June 1936 with a new name, the Santa Cruz County Fair & Rodeo Association. Thurber was elected president the following year and served through 1946. He had the sailor's penchant for having everything shipshape and demanded that chairmen get things done in a timely manner.

Craig Pottinger of the Nogales International wrote about the 1939 Fair, which was marred by rainy weather: "Numerous cars became stuck in the mud in the parking space about the main fair building. Bill Steen...pulled cars out of mud holes with a new 1940 Ford tractor," Pottinger wrote. "Persons attending the county fair dance Saturday night danced in about a half inch of mud, but liked it so well that at 1:00 a.m. a collection was taken up and the musicians played another hour." Pottinger ended by giving credit to H.B. Thurber, Dennis Hunt, Sy Swyers, Mrs. John Phillips, Ed LeGendre, and R.C. Larimore for their help in making the Fair a big success financially.

In the early 1950s, Mrs. Thurber became a semi-invalid. Dorothy Fisher, Mrs. Thurber's unmarried niece, moved to the ranch to help care for her. Dorothy taught school for a time in Tucson and then began teaching at the nearby Empire School, where she remained for many years until the school closed due to a decline in registrations in the mid-1960s.

Thurber was a founding member of the Patagonia/Sonoita Rotary Club. In 1974, George Yakobian, president of the Club at the time, invited Sen. Barry Goldwater to speak to the group at a luncheon at the Stage Stop. Goldwater flew in to Nogales Airport on the first leg of his re-election campaign, and was picked up at the edge of town by Anne Stradling, driving a horse drawn surrey. Also along for the ride were Yakobian and H. B. Thurber.

A crowd of about 100 people lined the streets as they pulled up in front of the Stage Stop Motel, when suddenly the horse spooked violently, knocking the buggy over on its side and dragging it down the street. Thurber, at age 77, still had the presence of mind to jump off to the left as the buggy tipped to the right. Goldwater was dumped out and Anne Stradling landed smack on top of him. An August 31, 1974, Arizona Republic article quoted Goldwater as joking, "I'd do this any day if she would fall on top of me."

Among the bystanders was cattleman Bob Bowman, who leaped to the rescue, grabbing the panicked horse and getting him under control. No one was seriously injured, and after being declared fit by Dr. Delmar Mock, Goldwater and party retired to the "Feedlot" dining room in the Stage Stop Motel where Yakobian encouraged his fellow Rotarians to "Vote Republican" in the upcoming election.

When Southern Pacific decided to abandon the railroad in 1960, Thurber negotiated the agreement whereby the Rotary Club took over ownership of the Patagonia Depot and eventually sold it to the Town of Patagonia for $1. Locals donated the money to renovate the building and move it several feet to comply with right of way legalities. The Depot continues to be a centerpiece of the town and a point of historical interest for locals and tourists alike.

In later years, Thurber sold the ranch to Bill and Penny Porter and built a house on an adjacent parcel, where he lived the rest of his life.

Southern Pacific Railroad operated in the area from 1882 until 1962. When the line was abandoned SP planned to demolish the Patagonia Depot. H.B. Thurber, president of the Patagonia/Sonoita Rotary Club, arranged for the building to be turned over to the Club. The landmark building was later sold to the Town of Patagonia for $1.
Photo courtesy Linda Donatelli and the Empire Ranch Foundation.

Jane Carrington modeling in a western fashion show put on by the Nogales and Patagonia Cowbelles. Jane Holbrook was chairman of the event, which was held at the new Patagonia High School in December of 1949. The evening included a potluck dinner and dance. A freezing winter rainstorm was not sufficient to dampen spirits as partygoers danced the night away to the tunes of Alvessa Hummel and her band. From left: Edith Farrell, Rose Pyeatt, Frank Hedgcock, Buster Pyeatt, Janie Carrington, Marie Schorr and Frances Hedgcock.
Photo courtesy Bowman Archives Center

Jane Tapper Carrington

Jane Tapper began a love affair with the Santa Rita Mountains the first moment she laid eyes on them in the late 1930s. She had left a career with Curtis Publishing Company in Chicago and come west to recuperate from a horseback riding accident. Once she saw the scenic Santa Ritas, she never looked back. Forty years later when she was terminally ill, she had her bed repositioned so she could look out the window and see her beloved mountains.

Jane, who was born in Illinois and had attended Smith College, was a single woman in her 30s when she first arrived in Sonoita. She registered as a guest at Hacienda Los Encinos, a working cattle/guest ranch operation owned by May and Neil Carr. Deciding she wanted to stay permanently in the area, Jane secured an administrative position with the Carrs and, as the consummate "people person," immediately became enmeshed in community activities.

A short time later, Charles Blake Carrington arrived in town with his son Chuck to finalize their purchase of approximately 8,000 acres of ranch property, plus Forest Service permits, and establish the Crown C Ranch. The property was a portion of the Empire Ranch, established by the Vail family in the late 1800s.

Although Jane was 20 years younger than Carrington and had many suitors, she fell madly in love with him and they were soon married in an intimate ceremony at Los Encinos. After a honeymoon in Hawaii they returned to the Crown C Ranch and began their life together.

Carrington was a successful businessman who had been appointed to the posi-

Jane Carrington at the Hacienda Los Encinos Guest Ranch where she worked as an assistant to the owners, Neil and May Carr. Jane came west to recuperate from a horseback riding accident, fell in love with Sonoita and never left. After Carr's tragic murder, Jane became a guardian to his children, John and Wendy. Ca. late 1930s.
Photo courtesy John Carr.

tion of Fire Commissioner of Newark, New Jersey. He presided over the Department while it went from a horse-drawn engine company to a motorized one, but his dream was to someday have a ranch like his relatives owned in Texas. After procuring the property, he divided the acreage into two ranches. He and his son, Chuck operated the Crown C, and his daughter and her husband ran the Lazy RR. Each ranch had approximately 4,000 patented acres plus Forest Service allotments.

They trucked their cattle out, originally shipping to a feedlot in Garden City, Kansas where Blake dealt with a man he greatly admired and respected. Later, he sent his cattle to an operation in Stanfield, Arizona, owned by movie star

Blake and Jane Carrington playing cribbage in front of the fireplace at the Crown C Ranch in Sonoita in the early 1940s.
Photo courtesy John Carr

John Wayne and Louis Johnson, a prominent cotton farmer in the area. Several movies, such as Broken Lance with Robert Wagner and Richard Widmark, and Oklahoma with Gordon McRae and Shirley Jones filmed some of their scenes on Crown C property.

Jane's nephew and godson, Bill Tollefson, remembers her as one of the kindest people he has ever known. "Any kindness I have comes to me through Janie," he said. Bill first came to Sonoita as a teenager in 1954. It was to be a weeklong visit, what his aunt referred to as a "quickie," but he too soon fell in love with southern Arizona. Jane told him, "This ranch is a business, Bill, not just way of life. It's day in and day out, your whole life experience." She placed him under the supervision of foreman Dick Jimenez and cowboy Aurelio Duran and told them to convert him from an easterner to a westerner.

Roundup at the Crown C. From left: Dick Jimenez, dehorning, Bill Tollefson, Janie Carrington, giving the shots. Joe Higgins (at right) is helping Bill hold the calf.
Photo courtesy Bill Tollefson

Bill said the Carringtons treated him like their own son, sending him to the University of Arizona and then on to veterinary school and buying him his first car, a 1949 Ford "Woody," that was his pride and joy. Jane also was there to help out when Neil Carr was senselessly murdered by a disgruntled employee at Los Encinos. Jane became guardian to the Carr's two children, John and Wendy, while Mrs. Carr tried to cope with the tragedy.

John Carr remembers a story Janie often told on herself when she wanted a smile. "Soon after Janie and Blake were married she went to Tucson on one of her shopping trips when she was still new to the ranching business. Blake asked her to get a gasket for the Kohler electric generator at Ronstadt Hardware Store. He gave her the part number and model number. When she got to the store she asked a fellow to help her carry this piece of equipment to her car. She didn't know what a gasket was, but figured it must be heavy since it was part of a machine. The cork gasket was about the size of a canning jar lid and probably weighed less than an ounce. She laughed and tipped the fellow a dollar as he carried it out to the car."

Tollefson said that Blake and Jane were a shining example of what love is all about. He remembered times when Jane, who was habitually late, didn't get back from Tucson at the time she had said she would be home. Blake would become agitated and by the time she got to the ranch he would be angry and red in the face. "She would breeze in and go up to him and pinch his cheek and say, 'Dear Blake, did you have a nice day?' The anger would just deflate out of him (sic)," Bill said.

Jane Carrington out on the ranch with her horse in the 1940s.
Photo courtesy John Carr.

This 1951 Ford truck advertising brochure was filmed in Adobe Canyon on the Crown C Ranch property in 1950.
Photo courtesy Bill Tollefson

In 1950, Ford Motor Company asked permission to shoot photos in the Adobe Canyon area of the ranch for an advertising brochure. Janie helped with the cattle work and was a horsewoman, but Blake was a gentleman rancher. Foreman Dick Jimenez had to give him a leg up on the horse for the photo shoot.

The cover featured an old windmill and a tin shed on the Crown C and the story was designed to demonstrate how useful a Ford truck would be on rugged ranch terrain.

Ford Truck Times Jan/Feb 1951
"Good Living on the Crown C"
by Barbara Sears
photos by Bill Sears

"Home in the rolling grasslands at the foot of the beautiful Santa Rita Mountains. Their life is a busy one. Acres of range need constant inspection, gates, fences, water places and equipment must be maintained and repaired.

During certain seasons there is concentrated work with the stock. Twice yearly the white-faced Herefords must be rounded up so that young calves can be branded, and vaccinated for black leg and the animals that are to be sold, separated and shipped. Most of the tasks are done by a small staff. A foreman and a cowboy handle range, cattle, and equipment with only occasional outside help.

The outside help comes during "gathering time," when all the neighbors turn to, country fashion, moving from ranch to ranch until everyone's stock is rounded up. Another example of working together is the teamwork between horses and mechanized equipment.

About noon the foreman's wife drives the truck to a prearranged location, loaded with good ranch beef, vegetables, salads, rolls, coffee, sometimes gingerbread and whipped cream, because riders who have been out since dawn have hearty appetites."

Blake Carrington passed away in 1963. Janie retained the ranch for several years with the help of Jimenez and his wife Eva, who did the cooking for the ranch. Aurelio Duran, who was married to Dick's sister, Victoria, was another longtime hand at the ranch. In 1970, Jane sold most of the property to Wood Canyon Development, retaining a portion for her family and a parcel for Dick and Eva Jimenez. She built a shop and garage for Jimenez and gave him the welding equipment saying, "Dick always loved welding. He should have it."

When Jane passed away, the family received a letter from a local resident saying, "We are moving out of the area. Sonoita without Janie just isn't Sonoita anymore." Bill Tollefson described her beautiful heart with this memory, "After she died, they found about $40,000 worth of IOU's in her safe in the basement. There was a note with the chits saying that they were to be destroyed upon her death."

The Crown C, now owned by Sydney Franklin, is still a working cattle ranch in 2008 and has added guest accommodations, a fitting tribute to the legacy left by a woman with a heart as big as the Santa Rita Mountains she so loved.

Jane Tapper Carrington was born in Sycamore, New York, Dec. 12, 1900.
Photo courtesy Bill Tollefson

Postcard of Bill Douglass and Roy Probasco walking downtown in Tucson in the 1940s. Photographers would snap pictures of pedestrians and by the end of the day they would be printed and posted on a board for sale. Postcard courtesy Billie Anna Douglass Gaskill

Brainard Allen "Bill" Douglass

"You can call me a rancher. You can call me a homesteader. You can call me a son-of-a-bitch. Just don't call me a cowboy," Bill Douglass often said. According to his daughter, Billie Anna Douglass (Gaskill), Bill thought of cowboys as drifters without a place of their own. He was proud of his two places, neighboring homesteads that he and his mother Elsa Douglass had "proved up" in Gardner and Fish Canyons near Sonoita.

Elsa had come west in 1896 when her husband, Robert Henry Douglass, M.D. contracted pleurisy and needed to move to a dry climate. They settled in Tucson with their three children Dorothy Jane, Brainard Allen, known as "Bill," and Gibson. Elsa was a nurse midwife and Robert Henry ran the Tucson railroad station because he was too ill to practice medicine.

Elsa was an excellent horsewoman and could go over jumps riding sidesaddle. She had trained a high-strung horse named Walter L to drive a buggy. Henry left the family and went to Mexico on a construction job for the railroad. Later Elsa drove Walter L and the buggy from Tucson to Imuris to meet with him. It was the last time that she would ever see Robert Henry. He had acquired another wife in Mexico and would not return to Arizona.

Robert Henry warned her that when she reached the border she should keep going straight ahead and not stop for anything because Pancho Villa's revolutionaries were roaming the area. The 50-mile trip back to Arizona took all night, from sundown to sunrise. Villas' troops were on the Sonora side of the border and as she passed with her horse and buggy two men began shooting at each other from opposite sides of the road behind her. She heard screaming as one man fell off the roof, apparently wounded. Elsa was tempted to turn around and attend to him, but saw that he was holding his rifle tightly across his chest as he rolled across the road. She remembered her husband's warning and urged her horse onward. Suddenly the supposedly wounded man leapt up and opened fire on his enemy. She had narrowly escaped the crossfire.

A picnic in Gardner Canyon with Bill Douglass (in foreground wearing hat) and his mother, Elsa, in the early 1900s. Elsa, called Nana by all the children, was an early homesteader in the area. This could be one of the Model A's Bill used for his bootlegging operations.
Photo courtesy Dori Randolph Kane and Billie Anna Douglass Gaskill.

Elsa and her son Bill decided to relocate in Sonoita in the early 1900s, where they filed on homesteads that had been abandoned by the original settlers. A prairie-style house had been built into the side of the hill on the property. It was always cool inside and the Douglasses used it for years to store food. The homesteads were registered in Elsa's name, although Bill and his family lived and worked on both of them.

One time Bill loaned an old miner $500 to work a placer claim north of Tucson. Every year the miner would pay off $50 or so, but eventually he stopped paying. When he came to Gardner Canyon, he would avoid the Douglass place. Bill went up to the mine and with the help of a 16-year-old kid, started making adobes from the clay there to build his house in Gardner Canyon. There was so much gold ore in the soil that when the light was right, the walls of the house glittered. Years later, when Billie Anna's son Bruce was about 10 or 12, he went up on the roof and dug out a little piece of adobe from the chimney. He panned it for gold and found a small ¼" nugget attached to a hunk of quartz. Billie Anna thought he was pretty clever, but his grandfather wasn't amused.

Bill lined the foundation on the porch of the Fish Canyon house with folding car hoods. You could open the hood and check under the house for snakes and varmints. During Prohibition, Bill hid his bootlegging still in there. He had other stills around the area and moved them often. One was on the hillside, one in Gardner Canyon, and yet another in the Mustangs. He used his Model A for his bootlegging operations. It was outfitted with a double gas tank. One side held gasoline and the other was filled with moonshine. Someone had informed on him and the sheriff stopped him and asked if he was transporting "hooch." Bill said, "Hell no, I'm on my way to Tucson on ranch business." While distracting the officer, he casually leaned down and flipped a switch that opened the divider and mixed the two liquids. The officer opened the gas cap, sniffed the fumes and tested the liquid with a dipstick before letting Bill go.

Bill planted crops and raised them Indian style, a method of dry farming that he had learned from the Papagos and Yaquis. They planted tall corn for the beans to climb on and the tomatoes and squash grew in the shade provided by the corn and beans. He pumped water from the windmill in Fish Canyon to one small spot in the garden. This ensured that they always had produce for their own kitchen even in times of drought.

At harvest time, he would spread out a tarp and throw on all the beans in a heap. It was fun for the kids to jump on the pile and trample the hulls off the beans before they sorted and picked them and poured them into new gunnysacks. They kept them for years, stacked on one side of the fireplace. The other side of the fireplace was reserved for family treasures and keepsakes.

Bill was sitting in the living room of the Gardner Canyon house one night in the late 1920s when someone shot at him through the window, narrowly missing him. The next day he made it a point to have lunch with the Mexican cowboys at

This is the first house that Elsa Douglass and her son, Bill, built on the homestead in Gardner Canyon. From left: Bill's children from an early marriage, Janie on a mule and Ralph on horseback His oldest son, Brainard, is not pictured. Ca. 1920s.
Photo courtesy Billie Anna Douglass Gaskill.

the Empire Ranch and told them the story in Spanish. There was a new cowboy, a drifter, at the table. Bill intimidated him with his anger over the incident and then got up and left. The stranger got spooked and was never seen again. Bill Douglass had no more trouble with people taking potshots at him. Soon afterwards, Bill made adobes, closed up the window and built a fireplace in that spot.

Douglass worked on all the John Wayne movies filmed in the area. He was the first person to be issued a union card to do wrangler work on the movies and also acted as an extra. He played a bit part as a rustler in Arizona, the movie that the Old Tucson Movie Studio was built for. Even when he was no longer able to ride, he was hired as the night watchman on location.

In 1936, Bill married his second wife, June Ruth Pettitt who was 27 years his junior. June's grandmother was a full-blooded Apache Indian who had been adopted by the Anderson family in Texas. Her daughter, Mattie, ran away from home with a man named Pettitt, who claimed to be related to Pettitt the Pirate,

Wranglers who worked on the movie, Red River, with John Wayne, Montgomery Clift, Joanne Dru and Walter Brennan, filmed in Elgin in 1946. They were responsible for the livestock, drove the wagons and did stunt work. Squatting in front of the stock trailer is Luke Randolph (father of Dori R. Kane). From left: Bill Douglass, Benny Ward and two cowboys. At right, Vernon Mounce. The picture was nominated for an Academy Award.
Photo courtesy Dori Randolph Kane and Billie Anna Douglass Gaskill.

a renegade whose boat went aground in the Gulf of Mexico, eluding capture by the British. When Pettit took up with another woman, he kicked out Mattie and their children, including June Ruth. Mattie ended up in Safford and the family was barely making ends meet when a visiting minister from the Seventh Day Adventist Church in Tucson helped them out and moved them to Ft. Lowell.

June and Bill had two daughters, Billie Anna and Dorothy. The Pima County line divided their two homesteads and the family moved back and forth, living

Brainard "Bill" Douglass, holding newborn Billie Anna, and his wife June Ruth Pettitt. June's father claimed to be a descendant of "Pettitt the Pirate," a renegade from a pirate ship that was chased by the English to New Orleans where the pirates emptied it of supplies and took off up the Mississippi. Ca 1937.
Photo courtesy of Billie Anna Douglass Gaskill.

Porch on the back of the Douglass house in Gardner Canyon. The small building in the rear was built into the hill. It was always cool inside and was used to store food. Standing back row: Billie Anna, Dorothy and their mother, June. Front row: Beverly Douglass (Bill's granddaughter) and Bill "Willie" Randolph, brother of Dori Kane. Billie Anna is holding "Bess" an Australian and Belgian Shepherd mix who lived to be 19 years old. Ca early 1940s.
Photo courtesy of Dori Kane and Billie Anna Douglass Gaskill

alternately in both. The one-room schools had to have a minimum number of children to hold classes, so the girls went to the Empire School in Pima County when it was low on registrations, and to the Sonoita School in Santa Cruz County, when they were needed there. Billie Anna went to first, second and seventh grades at Empire and third, fourth, fifth, and sixth at Sonoita. She says that some of the kids who caught the bus to school didn't have any shoes. She didn't want to wear them either but her father insisted, so she would walk to the bus stop and hang her shoes in the mesquite tree. When the bus dropped her off after school, she would retrieve her shoes wear them for the walk back home.

Douglass raised cattle and always had milk cows. During the summer Billie

Anna and Dorothy took charge of the entire milk cow operation, feeding, milking, and cleaning. They would separate the milk and take the milk and cream to the railroad in Sonoita to ship to Glendale, California for processing. The train returned with the empty cans, all scrubbed and ready to be refilled. Bill allowed the girls to keep the money, which would arrive by check shortly afterwards. For several years Bill and some partners imported cattle from Mexico. Sometimes a calf would be born on the truck while the mother was being shipped north. They would bring the calf to Sonoita and Billie Anna and Dorothy would hand feed and raise it.

Bill was always taking in people who needed help. A woman at the Arizona Children's Home knew of him and when a youngster was brought in who really needed a better chance, she would call Bill. He never said no.

One of these children was Willis Canady, who was charged with the dubious honor of watching over Billie Anna to make sure she still had her diapers on – they had to pin them to her clothes – and to see that she didn't wander off. Willis's brothers also came to the ranch and Billie Anna still remembers that someone threw Tom Canady's bike tire up in a tree where it hung for decades. Several years after Willis left their home, Billie Anna saw him at the Fair. She was about six years old and remembers being so happy to see him that she ran after him excitedly, calling out her pet name for him, "My Fatty, My Fatty." "Willis wasn't fat, but he was chunky and seemed big to me when I was a baby," Billie Anna explained.

Another boy Douglass took in was John Quirrin, a runaway who was caught stealing food from a bakery when he was about 15. Bill promised that he would turn him around and he did. John was very smart and could read Beowulf in two languages. He was a Master Sgt. and served as a sharpshooter in Germany and Japan in WWII, but couldn't become an officer because he had no proof of education past third grade.

Douglass also took in an older woman named Mrs. Owen. She lived in a little house in the rear and did some cooking and other work for Billie Anna's mother, June and her grandmother, Elsa. Mrs. Owen had dementia and when her children brought her new things to wear, she laid them carefully on the hillside. She considered them sacrifices that she was making to the Heavenly Father on behalf of her children.

When their old bull Papacito died, Bill left him to rot in the pasture where the coyotes and buzzards could get him. He considered that natural recycling, but

Mrs. Owen thought it was disrespectful to leave him where you could see him from the house. She rescued the skull and pelvic bone and put them in her room. She used a rod with a metal disc on it that she tapped to make a rhythmic noise and would chant prayers for the bull.

Billie Anna Douglass eavesdrops on the "man talk." From left Paul Heagle, Mr. Mitchell and Bill Douglass. Ca 1944 – 1946.
Photo courtesy Billie Anna Douglass Gaskill

Bill often went to Mexico on cattle buying trips. While there he had an affair with a young señorita, the daughter of his best rancher friend. June found out about it and Bill brought her many gifts as peace offerings. One was Saino, a horse who didn't like men or children. June trained him and rode him everywhere, but he never adjusted to the altitude and they had to send him to friends in Tucson. Another gift was a young cow that ended up suffering from screwworms because vaqueros had branded famous brands all over her body, even her face. By the time she got to Sonoita, she had burned skin curling and peeling from about 15 places. He also brought June a ring, necklace and bracelet and took her to Nogales to be fitted for red boots that she could wear riding or dancing. June never forgave him, and when Billie Anna was 14 and Dorothy was 11, she left him and the children.

According to Bailey Foster, who married Bill's youngest daughter Dorothy, "Bill had a heart as big as all outdoors, but he couldn't show his tender side. He thought that would show weakness. When it came to kids, drunks, old livestock, he'd go the distance. One day he asked me to go with him to Tucson to look for Red Craig. Red was an alcoholic and Bill heard that he was in a bad way. We brought him back to Bill's place where he stayed till he sobered up."

Dori Randolph (Kane) was another one of the "Douglass kids." She remembers Bill with respect and affection. She took to ranch life and when she was 19, she came back and worked as a cowgirl on the ranch. She says that she owes him so much for taking her into his home and raising her with his two daughters who became her lifelong friends.

Irvin Douglas with his children in the mid-1920s. From left front row: Irvin and his daughter, Olive. Back row: Irvin "Dick," Volney and Grace.
Photo courtesy Rene Prentice

Maude Jacobs Douglas
Olive Douglas Stoddard

"Mama insisted on locating the house by the only growing thing above the grass, a lone tall yucca plant," Olive Douglas Stoddard said in her memoirs. Maude and Irvin Douglas homesteaded near Sonoita around 1906, in an area now known as Yucca Ash Road. They lived in a tent with their year-old baby, Grace, and the following year a son, Volney Marx was born.

"There was no doctor for miles and Mama used a chair to pull upon. She said doctors were a nuisance when having a baby anyway." Three years later Olive was also born in the tent, with the help of another chair. There was no crib for the babies and Maude slept with them lying on her breast.

Maude and Irvin were married in Yuma, Dec. 20, 1903. He was 42 and Maude was 23. Irvin had a bad heart and they decided to move to Arizona for the healthful climate. They settled near the army camp at Ft. Lowell in Tucson and ran a boarding house there. Maude's 12-year-old sister, Grace Jacobs, came to live with them. She attended school and also helped with the boarders. Irvin's sister-in-law, Myrtle Kilpatrick, also came to stay and work with them.

Grace and Myrtle moved to Sonoita with the Douglas family. Maude's life on the homestead was not an easy one. She did the laundry in a washtub over a fire. The white clothes had to be boiled and she scrubbed them on a washboard. The good clothing was cotton and had to be ironed with a flatiron heated on the wood stove.

All the food was homemade, including bread. The women would gather wild grapes to make jelly and made white fudge from wild black walnuts. "At Easter time Mama would take little scraps of colored cloth and wrap eggs with them, tying them on with string, then boiling them. They would come out all bright colored patterns," Olive said.

To "prove up" their homestead, Irvin and Maude were required to build a home on the land and plant crops. Irvin cut posts from the big juniper trees on the property and fenced the garden to protect it from the livestock on the open range. He bought a cow and chickens and put in a crop of corn. Maude, with the help of Grace, Myrtle and some neighbors, dug a 40' well by hand. Irvin built a dam to turn water from Gardner Canyon to his fields over a mile away. He hitched a team to an iron scoop with iron handle to fill and dump dirt.

The rains were plentiful in the early years and in addition to the corn, Irvin planted and harvested pinto beans and garbanzos, with cantaloupe, watermelons, pumpkins and turnips planted along the crops edges. The neighbors all came to help at harvest time and Maude cooked for all the workers.

Irvin had done some assaying for miners in the area and staked a claim at the north end of the Santa Rita Mountains that he called the "Reeta." Olive remembered several occasions when her parents loaded up the buckboard wagon with bedding and food and went over to their mining claim to try panning a bit of gold.

Sometime around 1915, Lily Douglas, the widow of Irvin's brother, Rob, came to the homestead to help out. Rob had died young and left her with four children. One day the women were working in the well. Lily was down at the bottom, filling the bucket with wet dirt. When it was ready, she would holler and someone would pull it up. Myrtle's little sister, Rosa, was turning the windlass to pull the bucket up when it slipped from her hands and plummeted down the well, landing on Lily's head and splitting her scalp open.

Grace climbed into the well and pinched the edges of the wound together to stop the bleeding. They waited in the bottom of the well for over an hour while Myrtle ran for help. It took several more hours for the long trip by wagon to get to the doctor in Tucson. Lily was ill for years afterwards and relatives helped out with her children. Five-year-old Warren moved in with Maude and Irvin.

Olive remembered her mother's love of nature and the many lessons she taught her children. "When I was about four years old, she took us four children out on a warm, clear night, lay down on the ground and told us to lie with our heads to hers, like a wheel. Then she pointed out the immensity of space, the "Big Dipper,"

The Douglas family children on a visit to their Aunt Grace in California. From left: Volney, Olive, Dick, Grace and Aunt Grace. Two youngsters in front are Aunt Grace's children. Mid-1920s.
Photo courtesy Rene Prentice

and many planets. I felt the humility of it all so much, I've never forgotten.

"One day she climbed about 15 feet up a big ash tree in Gardner Canyon, about half a mile from our house. She was wearing an ankle-length skirt and heavy work shoes that the farmwomen wore. She took a baby hawk, covered with fuzzy down, out of the nest and carried him down in a flour sack. We had a good look, and then she climbed back up and returned him to his nest."

While Maude was busy at her sewing machine, she would listen to the children recite their multiplication tables. "If we acted up and did not behave, she had a little willow switch by her hand, to remind us. I don't recall that she ever used it on us, but she washed my sister's mouth out with a bar of laundry soap for using bad language," Olive said. She played the violin and the piano, and had one of the first grand pianos that ever came to Tucson. Occasionally Irvin played the violin while Maude would chord on the piano for the schoolhouse dances. Families would put their children to sleep on quilts in the back of the wagons and dance all night, getting home in time to do the chores before breakfast.

Around 1918, Rosa moved to Nevada where her husband got a job in the mines. They wrote to Irvin that the mine was hiring, so the Douglas family decided to join them. They hitched up the buckboard and team to drive to the train station in Tucson. Olive said, "On the way we took chickens in a wire cage for some friends. The wagon went through a rough washout. A hen had laid an egg, and it rolled out of the cage onto the wagon bed and broke. Papa kept going, but Mama said, 'It's good food, we mustn't waste it.' Papa said "It's good, so you eat it." So Mama opened her mouth and dumped the raw egg in, swallowed it and almost gagged."

When they arrived in Searchlight, Nevada, they found Rosa Kennedy bedridden with the flu. There was an influenza epidemic in the camp and soon Maude found herself nursing many of the miners and their families. Rosa and one of her children died and Maude took in two of the children. Olive said, "It was cold in the little canvas house. Papa put a mattress on the floor in the living room, the center of the house, and Mama slept there with the two children. Little Irvin was on the old couch across the room. My brother Volney and Papa were on the right side of the blanket curtain in the little bedroom. Grace and I slept on the floor in the left side of bedroom."

One cold night in January while Maude was sleeping with the two little Kennedy children on the floor in the living room, she heard a noise in the kitchen and got up. A shot rang out. Maude was killed instantly by a shotgun blast to the heart and fell back almost on top of the children on the floor. "I thought I heard a banging before she screamed," Olive said. "The burglar had stacked a circle of groceries just outside the kitchen door, the way an Indian prepares them to carry. Evidently when Mama screamed he realized what he had done and left the premises so fast he left the groceries behind."

The sheriff got a posse and hunting dogs and followed the tracks. The renegade Indian had a limp, but the country was so rocky and rugged, they lost the tracks. Years later they found a skeleton in a cave with many guns and other things he had stolen. Equipment and belongings of two cowboys who had been shot after Maude were also found in the cave.

Sisters Olive and Grace Douglas in the mid-1920s.
Photo courtesy Rene Prentice

After Maude's death, Irvin took the oldest boy, Volney, back to the homestead in Sonoita with him. Volney, who was about nine at the time, told his son Mark that they lived like bachelors, surviving on beans and biscuits. Rather than wash dishes, they wiped the plates off with the remaining bread and turned them upside down to dry. Volney said that raising beans was backbreaking work, planting, harvesting, hulling and then filling 100 pound gunney sacks that they would haul to Greaterville to sell. After a year of hard labor, their total reward was a cartridge shell with a tiny bit of gold powder in the bottom.

The other children were split up and Olive went to live with an aunt in Yuma for several years. They all eventually joined their father and brother in Sonoita. They went to Patagonia High School and Irvin would drive them to Sonoita to catch the school bus. Most of the time, the old Model T wouldn't start and Irvin would hitch up the horses and pull the car to get it started.

Olive married Emory Stoddard when she was 17 years old and after ranching in Tombstone and trying to make a living running a butcher shop, they came back to her father's homestead. Emory was often gone on business and Olive said that she did a lot of the ranch work, raising hogs, helping with the branding and growing beans. They lived in the original house built by Irvin, roofed with metal and wood siding from the abandoned Post Office at Greaterville and still warmed by a wood stove.

Olive Douglas on Brewster at the Empire Ranch. 1924.
Photo courtesy Rene Prentice

Luz Encinas Caviglia and Angelo Caviglia on their first wedding anniversary in 1916. Angelo was the son of Bernardo and Pastora Vega Caviglia. Photo courtesy Arthur Caviglia

Angelo Caviglia
Arthur Caviglia

"It's time for a fiesta!" The voice of Don Jacinto, the popular Tucson radio personality, floated across the airwaves with the news. There was another exciting tardeada, horse race, dance and barbecue planned at Angelo Caviglia's restaurant, bar and dance hall in Arivaca. Angelo's fiestas, held regularly during the boom years at the nearby Ruby Mine, were eagerly anticipated events in the 1930s and people traveled from miles around to join in the fun.

"My father would buy a cord of wood and build a big fire in a pit. He covered the coals with rocks and set the beef in cans or sacks on top. Then he would lay a big piece of tin over it and seal the whole thing with a huge mound of dirt. It looked like a grave to us kids," said one of Angelo's sons, Arthur Caviglia.

The beef would roast for a day or two before the fiesta. And what a feast it was. Along with the barbecued beef and potato salad, there were tortillas, salsa and beans, all homemade by local Mexican ladies. It was "All you can eat," for a $1 a plate.

In a flat stretch of ground under the trees at Alamo Park that ran along a nearby wash, they made a track for horse races and put on rodeos, with roping events and bucking horses. The branches of the trees made natural benches that people could sit on to watch the action.

The Caviglias lived next door to the bar and dance hall and had several acres in back where Angelo raised and bred Thoroughbreds, including Billy, his prize stud. Billy had a well-earned reputation as a winner and one day Angelo accepted a challenge from a Mexican rancher to race against his mare in Sonora. When Billy won, the rancher took out his anger on the mare and Angleo decided never to race there again.

Frank Mendoza (right) holds Billy, Caviglia's top stud and racehorse. March 20, 1939.
Photo courtesy Arthur Caviglia

Musicians came from Tucson to play for the dances. Art remembers one of his mother's friends, an unmarried lady who loved to dance and never missed one of the fiestas. She wore a lot of makeup and fancy clothes and drove a new car that always had a large bedpan on the back seat. It was a long drive home in the dark and she told them, "I'm not getting down on the desert to pee on the way home. There are too many snakes around."

Angelo was born in Arivaca, the son of an Italian immigrant, Bernardo Caviglia, who homesteaded in what is now Arivaca Lake in 1887. Bernardo married Pastora Vega from Arivaca and after only ten months and 12 days of marriage, Pastora died giving birth to Angelo in 1894. The single father enlisted the help of local women as wet nurses for the baby and remained a widower for the rest of his life. He bought the Rita Mora homestead east of Arivaca, where they lived

(Left) Lencho Leon showing Nellie, a mare sired by Angelo's top stud, Billy, (right) held by Candido Aroz, who worked for Bernardo. Photo taken at the informal racetrack Caviglia built in Arivaca. Ca. 1930s.
Photo courtesy Arthur Caviglia

for several years, and built the grocery store in Arivaca.

According to Arthur, "My grandfather was tight with his money. He saved and bought land. He owned the Calera Ranch, northeast of Arivaca, and built a pond there called Caviglia Dam that is still shown on maps. The pond never dries up. He also had holdings in Tucson, including the Parkview Hotel. Every so often he would hitch up the horse and buggy and drive to Tucson or Nogales to check on his properties. I can still picture him walking down the street, bent over, with his hands clasped behind his back. My brother Albert and I were about four and six at the time. We thought it was fun to follow behind him and mimic his walk."

Formal portrait of Bernadina Caviglia of Genoa, Italy, the matriarch of the Caviglia family. Her sons Angelo and Bernardo immigrated to the United States in 1876. Bernardo homesteaded in Arivaca in 1887. His brother, Angelo, owned the Double Stamp Saloon in Tucson and had bars in Bisbee and the Clifton-Morenci area.
Photo courtesy Arthur Caviglia

Small children play near the windmill at Caviglia's La Calera Ranch. Ca. 1927.
Photo courtesy Arthur Caviglia

Angelo was quite different from his father. As a youngster, he was a handful and his father sent him to St. Michael's School in Santa Fe to shape him up. "It didn't work," according to Art. He retained his fun loving spirit and good nature throughout his life. He married Luz Encinas from Oro Blanco and they had five children, four boys and one girl. Angelo waited until his father, Bernardo, a tee-totaler, passed away in 1932 before he built the bar, restaurant and dance hall he named Caviglia's Café. He also installed a gas pump in front of their house. Caviglia felt fortunate to have a Kohler plant to generate electricity. Many of the homes in the area had no electricity or running water.

Angelo was kind hearted and generous. "If someone died and didn't have any funds, he would furnish the lumber to make a coffin. He loaned his truck to people to go to the doctor and let them run tabs in the grocery when money was short," Art said. When the family moved to Tucson in the early '40s, Angelo forgave many debts from the store.

There were about 100 to 200 ranchers and vaqueros living in the Arivaca area when Art grew up there in 1930s. There were another 2,500 miners and families living in a tent city in nearby Ruby. The tents had wood floors, canvass sides and a tin roof and the luxury of running water, but no indoor bathroom facilities. Ruby had its own school and Art and his siblings watched movies there when they were teenagers.

Art went to the two-room Arivaca School for the first eight grades. There were about fifty students in the school. One room was for grades one through five, the other for sixth through eighth graders. The teachers stayed in a guesthouse during the week and went home on weekends. Helen Noon was his first teacher and later he had Mrs. Reed.

Once a year the priest from Santa Cruz Church in Tucson came to Arivaca and Sasabe and to towns across the border to baptize babies and perform other sacraments such as weddings, first communions and confirmations. Luz Caviglia had a high table built that was set up in their home and served as an altar for the priest to say Mass during his stay.

Art remembers that they had milk cows, cattle and about 200 chickens when he was growing up. He delivered the milk for .10 cents a quart and got to keep the money. During the fiestas, Art made Sno Cones, or Cimarrones and sold them for a nickel. There weren't any organized activities for children, but the creek ran clear and they could swim. There was an orchard where they climbed the trees to get green apples and pears.

Angelo Caviglia (center) sent this postcard to his sweetheart, Luz Encinas, dated September 22, 1914. They were married the following year.
Postcard courtesy Arthur Caviglia.

When they had bailes at his father's place, Art would ride his bike all over town inviting the girls to come to the dance. A jukebox played tunes for a quarter. Art's wife, Angela, says he always picked a tall girl to dance with so he could put his hand on her "butt." "And I wouldn't hesitate to do it again," Art added.

Sometimes Art's older sister, Bernardina, would borrow the car and drive them to Sasabe where they would pick up their friends, the Escalante children. Then they crossed the border to the little town of El Mesquite and head for La Posabita, a bar and dance hall. There was a big cement platform where people danced and roller-skated. They had no refrigeration, so they kept the beer in a big can and lowered it into the well to keep it cool. When someone wanted a drink, they would pull it up. Art is sure his parents never found out about these escapades.

Arivaca did not have a high school, so after eighth grade the children lived in Tucson at a house their father bought near Five Points, on Sixth Avenue. A lady named Matilda stayed with them during the week and they went home to Arivaca on weekends. When the Ruby Mine shut down in the early '40s, Caviglia sold the ranch and his business and moved his family to Tucson where there were better financial opportunities and the children could complete their schooling.

Arthur Caviglia in his army uniform in Hanau, Germany. November 8, 1951.
Photo courtesy Arthur Caviglia

Bibliography

Barnes, Will C., *Arizona Place Names,*" University of Arizona Press, 1988.

Benjamin, Stan, *Patagonia, Arizona,* Benjamin and Company, 2001.

Chapman, Grace Kane, *Arizona National Pioneer Ranch Histories,* Vol. VIII.

Conover, Adele, *Keepers of the Range, The Story of the Arizona Cattle Growers' Association,* Heritage Publishers, LLC, 2007.

Fowler, Charles: *"Santa Cruz Valley Roundup,"* Nogales International November 12, 1986.

Kane, Mary Gardner, *Reminiscences,* told to Effie L. Scott and Mrs. George F. Kitt, 1926.

Martin, Donnie Lewis, *Laura and Blain Lewis,* Arizona National Ranch Histories of Living Pioneer Stockmen, Compiled by Betty Accomazzo. Vol. VII, 1985

Piper, Posy, *History of Ranching in Santa Cruz County Arizona,* Santa Cruz County Cowbelles Ranchers' Heritage Center, 2004.

Tetzloff, R. W., *Thomas Gardner, Arizona Pioneer,* San Diego Corral of the Westerners, The Wrangler, Vol. 15, 1982

Whetzel, Mary Wiley: *Echoes Down the Centuries,* iUniverse Inc.2007.

Wood, Tom and Joan Kane, *The Other Side of the Mountain,* Tom Wood Books, 2007.

Index

D

E

F

G

H

J

K

L

M

N

O

P

Q

R

S

T

U

V

W

Y

Printed in the United States
132910LV00002B/1/P

9 780979 026133